Fighting and Negotiating with Armed Groups:
The difficulty of securing strategic outcomes

Samir Puri

Fighting and Negotiating with Armed Groups:
The difficulty of securing strategic outcomes

Samir Puri

IISS The International Institute for Strategic Studies

The International Institute for Strategic Studies

Arundel House | 13–15 Arundel Street | Temple Place | London | WC2R 3DX | UK

First published July 2016 **Routledge**
4 Park Square, Milton Park, Abingdon, Oxon, OX14 4RN

for **The International Institute for Strategic Studies**
Arundel House, 13–15 Arundel Street, Temple Place, London, WC2R 3DX, UK
www.iiss.org

Simultaneously published in the USA and Canada by **Routledge**
270 Madison Ave., New York, NY 10016

Routledge is an imprint of Taylor & Francis, an Informa Business

© 2016 The International Institute for Strategic Studies

DIRECTOR-GENERAL AND CHIEF EXECUTIVE Dr John Chipman
EDITOR Dr Nicholas Redman
EDITORIAL Alice Aveson, Jill Lally, James Middleton, Nancy Turner
COVER/PRODUCTION John Buck

The International Institute for Strategic Studies is an independent centre for research, information and debate on the problems of conflict, however caused, that have, or potentially have, an important military content. The Council and Staff of the Institute are international and its membership is drawn from almost 100 countries. The Institute is independent and it alone decides what activities to conduct. It owes no allegiance to any government, any group of governments or any political or other organisation. The IISS stresses rigorous research with a forward-looking policy orientation and places particular emphasis on bringing new perspectives to the strategic debate.

The Institute's publications are designed to meet the needs of a wider audience than its own membership and are available on subscription, by mail order and in good bookshops. Further details at www.iiss.org.

Printed and bound in Great Britain by Bell & Bain Ltd, Thornliebank, Glasgow

British Library Cataloguing in Publication Data
A catalogue record for this book is available from the British Library

Library of Congress Cataloging in Publication Data

ADELPHI series
ISSN 1944-5571

ADELPHI 459
ISBN 978-1-138-23856-5

Contents

The strategic art of confronting armed groups

For states, it is acutely important to master the strategic art of dealing with non-state armed groups. Most wars of the past 30 years have been intra-state, albeit with varying amounts of outside interference. Often, a point comes when the governments involved conclude that military victory is not imminent and so attempt to open some sort of political track. Even after this realisation, securing a satisfactory outcome is hard. States can fail to articulate achievable long-term objectives. And they can fail to formulate and implement a strategy that marries coercive measures with political overtures. Many states find themselves wandering a strategic wilderness, neither winning on the battlefield nor resolving the conflict at the negotiating table.

There are several permutations of fighting and talking with armed groups. In some instances, states have fought, negotiated and then fought again. In other instances states have fought and negotiated simultaneously. Some states facing multiple armed groups have adopted a discriminatory approach, fighting some while negotiating with others. Every war features a unique interplay between security measures and political engagement – but the interplay is always present.

This is hardly a revelation. It ought to be the bedrock of sound strategic thinking. The pertinent question is *how* they overlap in the wars of today, and what implications this carries for policymakers. Conflicts with armed groups risk becoming generational undertakings, scarring the globe in wars that have no apparent end in sight. And yet, since all wars end eventually, it is worth exploring how to avoid vacillating between the military and political tracks of engagement, with no discernible outcome on the horizon. Conversely, what constitutes effective and realistic strategy towards armed groups?

Since the end of the Cold War, purely inter-state wars have been relatively rare. Examples include the First Gulf War (1991), India–Pakistan (1998), the US invasion of Iraq (2003), and Russia–Georgia (2008). Armed groups featured even in some of these wars, and one (Iraq 2003) gave birth to a nasty insurgency. Over the same period, intra-state conflict has been much more prevalent, affecting Europe, Latin America, North Africa, sub-Saharan Africa, central and south Asia, Southeast Asia, and the Middle East. Examples include the former Yugoslavia, Colombia, Libya, the Democratic Republic of the Congo (DRC), Pakistan, the Philippines and Yemen. Of course, not all of these conflicts have been waged within the borders of a single state and without any external involvement. The US blamed Iran for stoking Iraq's post-2003 civil war. India accused Pakistan of using proxies to fight on its behalf. Russia, too, has pursued its aims by backing, for example, Ukraine's separatists. Western states also selectively back armed groups, such as the Kosovo Liberation Army's secessionist war against Serbia (1999), the Afghan Northern Alliance's war to change the Taliban regime (2001), and the Kurdish Peshmerga's fight against the Islamic State, also known as ISIS or ISIL, from 2014. Yet most conflicts have in essence been intra-state struggles.

A canny armed group will do what it can to blunt the impact of a government's use of military force. It might hide among the populace or base itself in inaccessible terrain. Security forces may struggle to target the group and may never be able to corner it. Even inflicting losses on the group may not prove decisive, especially if civilians are hurt or harassed in the process. Imprisoning a killing group's leaders may not force its collapse either, if others are keen to pick up the leadership mantle. If the group operates in a decentralised manner, with its units spread out so that the loss of one does not spell the end of its cause, this too can enhance its survivability. A weakened armed group can scatter, bide its time and renew its challenge later on, so long as its ideology retains sway, and it can continue to finance itself.

In conflicts where military victory has been elusive, states may explore the possibility of negotiations – albeit in conjunction with security measures. Some states sincerely explore the possibilities for peace, offering to include the group in national political processes if it renounces violence. Other states simply negotiate to buy time, to blunt international criticism or to placate allies. They may use talks to gain intelligence about the group and to try to cause its fracture. All the while, the armed group may also be playing for time, sending negotiators who do not speak for the hardliners while the violence rages.

Some armed-group foes are so implacable that there is no basis for a negotiated solution. And other groups are so atomised or disorganised that a negotiating partner cannot be identified, and there is little point in engaging them. Foreign sponsors of armed groups are a serious issue, as are neighbouring states that are not actively intervening, but may be turning a blind eye to safe havens.

All of these factors contribute to the difficulties of opening viable talks, and compound the obstacles political leaders face in selling negotiations to deeply aggrieved people on all the sides. Former British prime minister Tony Blair could never forget the 3,500 people who died in Northern Ireland's conflict as he pushed for a deal with Sinn Féin.[1] This pales in comparison to the 220,000 people who are estimated to have died in Colombia's five-decade-long war with the Revolutionary Armed Forces of Colombia (FARC), leaving President Juan Manuel Santos an even bigger task.[2]

These complications only multiply when states are working in coalitions abroad, in support of host governments such as Iraq, Afghanistan and the DRC. Here, for interveners and host governments, there are fundamental choices to be made over whether or not to include the various armed groups in the political processes that are taking root.

Fighting armed groups is an uncertain business, and so is negotiating. Doing both, alternately, concurrently or selectively, is highly demanding. Variations of this challenge have exasperated states the world over. A study on Turkey's response to the Kurdistan Workers' Party (PKK) observed: 'Research on conflict resolution and counterterrorism rarely seems to consider the relationship between the two processes.'[3] This is the matter of concern here. How do measures that seek to degrade the capabilities of armed groups and to defeat them militarily interplay with measures that seek disarmament, negotiation and conflict-resolution outcomes? How do they pull against each other? And to what ultimate ends are they being employed?

Northern Ireland is sometimes held up as a textbook case of overcoming these difficulties in pursuit of a negotiated end. British military force was used to stabilise the security situation, to coerce the Provisional Irish Republican Army (IRA) into coming to the negotiating table, and then to protect the peace process as it gained momentum. Sri Lanka took a very different path in its struggle with the Tamil Tigers: after several ceasefires and unsuccessful efforts to negotiate a political solution, the government used overwhelming force to destroy its opponent on the battlefield. Yet in neither case was the route to resolution clear or straightforward to the respective government or the expert community. This serves to underline the difficulty for any government in using a combination of negotiations and military force to bring a conflict to what it considers to be an acceptable conclusion.

The examples of Northern Ireland and Sri Lanka are unusual in that governments were able to bring the conflicts to a conclusion, rather than simply containing them through a mixture of negotiation and coercion. Many governments have to settle for an intermediate objective. The table below distinguishes the genuinely strategic outcomes that states may ultimately desire from the practical outcomes that they are more likely to attain.

Table 1. **Goal moderation when confronting armed groups**

	Moderated Goal	Desired Goal
Security outcome	Containment	Destruction
Political outcome	Ceasefire	Peace deal

An avowed desire to achieve a given outcome – be it eliminating an armed group or politically accommodating it – may not be feasible in the immediate term. This tempering may represent a precursor goal to a victory that comes years or even decades later. But it is perhaps more likely to become a stopping point in its own right.[4]

It is tough for policymakers to remain consistent in their objectives when conflicts can last decades. U-turns taken to avoid dead ends are all too common. Master plans rarely survive contact with the realities of war. This is why good strategy can facilitate adaptive responses to changing situations. For practitioners, improvisation is crucial. Wars unfold viscerally, unpredictably and confusingly. Armed groups will do all they can to avoid being pinned down by states, whether on the battlefield or in talks.

This book seeks to develop a framework to help analysts and policymakers understand the challenges of using a combination of coercion and diplomacy in dealing with non-state armed groups. From there, it will consider which complexities have proved most inhibiting and which have been worked around. Can the competing logics be reconciled? What are the obvious traps that states fall into? What appear to be the smarter moves? Does the adoption of a particular combination of force and diplomacy close off the option of using other combinations in the future? And, to arrive at an acceptable end state, how much flexibility do states need in the objectives they seek?

To answer these questions, the book will consider a number of cases of intra-state conflict. They vary considerably with regard to geography, the number and type of participants, the objectives of the protagonists, and the mix of force and diplomacy employed over time. The cases also vary by outcome. Every war features a unique interplay between security measures and political engagement – but the interplay is always present.

The purpose of casting the net so wide is to strengthen the conclusions that we can draw. For each case, the book will analyse objectives and methods, and chart how these changed over time. It is the author's intention that by doing so, the lessons for strategy can be made explicit, rather than getting lost amid a bloody contemporary history of wars involving armed groups.

Notes

1 Simon Rogers, 'Deaths in the Northern Ireland Conflict since 1969', *Guardian*, 10 June 2010, http://www.theguardian.com/news/datablog/2010/jun/10/deaths-in-northern-ireland-conflict-data.

2 National Centre for Historical Memory, 'Armed Conflict in Colombia Statistics', http://www.centrodememoriahistorica.gov.co/micrositios/informeGeneral/estadisticas.html.

3 Ersel Aydinli and Nihat Ali Ozcan, 'The Conflict Resolution and Counterterrorism Dilemma: Turkey Faces its Kurdish Question', *Terrorism and Political Violence*, vol. 23, no. 3, 2011, p. 438.

4 Stopping points are a useful way of thinking about what a strategy can achieve in practice: Thomas C. Schelling, *Arms and Influence* (New Haven, CT: Yale University Press, 1966), p. 135.

CHAPTER ONE

The difficulties of accommodating or eliminating armed groups

After 30 years of troubles, thousands of deaths, Northern Ireland ... its daily life scarred ... by sectarian bitterness ... we agreed to shape a new future. Enemies would become not just partners in progress but sit together in government. People who used to advocate the murder of British ministers and security services, would be working with them.

Tony Blair, 2002[1]

In 30 years the LTTE [Liberation Tigers of Tamil Eelam] has killed many people. When I won the presidential election in 2005 there were LTTE police stations in the north and east. There were Tiger courts. What was missing was only a Tiger parliament. Today we have finished all that forever.

Mahinda Rajapaksa, 2009[2]

Many states aspire to end their confrontations with armed groups, but a decisive outcome can be painstakingly hard to secure. This is true whether a state is working towards politically accommodating an armed group or towards its elimination. Northern Ireland and Sri Lanka are, respectively, examples of what this can involve. One must not assume that the UK's engagement of the Provisional Irish Republican Army (IRA) was predetermined to end in an agreement with its political wing, Sinn Féin, or that the destruction of the Liberation Tigers of Tamil Eelam (LTTE) was similarly predetermined. Each was a protracted saga in which the policy response repeatedly slipped into lethargy, in the face of a seemingly intractable challenge. How did the UK overcome this to use the various strands of its response to secure a political outcome? Conversely, how did Sri Lanka's mixture of responses culminate in a violent outcome?

Northern Ireland: the UK politicises its security response

One must never judge the nature of a scenario solely by how it ends. The story of UK strategy in Northern Ireland is one of missteps, setbacks, and trial and error. It is also a story of evolution. Beginning as a security response, it slowly broadened into a peace process involving the very armed group that had fought to end British rule in Northern Ireland. The British government pursued its political strategy tentatively at first, fighting the IRA while covertly seeking dialogue. After many false starts, and amid continued bloodshed, negotiations gathered sufficient momentum to become the centrepiece of British strategy, albeit always in conjunction with security measures.

The 1998 Good Friday Agreement was the culmination of the process of persuading the IRA to abandon its armed struggle and decommission its weapons. In exchange, its leaders would participate in Northern Irish politics, the British Army would reduce its presence and Northern Ireland would receive greater economic investment from London. Along the way, rejectionists who were opposed to talking to London and wanted to carry on the fight would splinter from the IRA. But the core of the IRA underwent a metamorphosis, under the auspices of Sinn Féin, to become a predominantly political rather than military actor.

This outcome has led to debate over what lessons can emerge for 'talking to terrorists'. According to one argument, the UK had all but defeated the IRA, and the 'terms of the dialogue between the British government and the IRA were set by the war that preceded it'.[3] Contending interpretations empha-sise the ameliorative process of dialogue and trust building.[4] Whichever argument one leans towards, it is clear that both fighting and talking played a role in how the conflict devel-oped. The focus here is on examining the symbiosis between the different elements of the UK's response, and on its evolving policy mix. The British state's early realisation of the primacy of politics in managing the conflict was overshadowed by the pressing nature of the security threat. As is explained here, it took three decades to tangibly rebalance the policy mix, and to give a definitively political character to what had initially been a security response.

The predominance of war and the tentativeness of politics (1969–1989)

British involvement in Ireland has had a long, troubled history. Ireland ceased to be a British colony in 1921 when the Anglo-Irish Treaty granted it dominion status. However, not all of Ireland wanted independence. Under pressure from union-ists, including the paramilitary Ulster Volunteer Force (UVF), Northern Ireland was allowed to opt out of the new Irish state. The result was partition. Unionist-dominated authori-ties ruled six Irish counties from Belfast, and Dublin ruled 26. In subsequent decades, while Northern Ireland remained in the UK, it became progressively less economically and strategically vital to London. It only returned to prominence in the UK's political agenda when intercommunal violence escalated between unionists (members of the Protestant community, looking to the UK for legitimacy and protection) and republicans (members of the Catholic community who wanted to end British rule).[5] Violence peaked in 1969, heralding an era referred to as 'the Troubles'.

The British Army was deployed that year under *Operation Banner*. Its aim was to bolster the police force, the Royal Ulster Constabulary (RUC), and restore order. British soldiers were initially welcomed, even by Catholics, as a stabilising influence, but soon became targets for retribution when republicans portrayed them as unionist puppets.[6] Taking up the mantle of violent republicanism, a new generation of Provisional IRA members split in 1969 from the Official IRA, which had been unprepared for the Troubles. The Provisional IRA (hereafter referred to as the IRA) would fight to end what it denounced as British colonial occupation – a cause that was galvanised by overreactions in British tactics. On what came to be known as Bloody Sunday on 30 January 1972, British soldiers killed 14 people who had been marching against policies such as the internment without trial of hundreds of suspected republican paramilitaries.

British prime minister Edward Heath (1970–74) in March 1972 initiated direct rule of Northern Ireland from London, fearing the eruption of civil war amid escalating intercommunal killings in the wake of Bloody Sunday. Direct rule was an admission that Northern Ireland could no longer be governed from Stormont (Belfast's seat of government). It validated republican portrayals of British colonialism and it ended unionist control by transferring power to the Northern Ireland Office (NIO) and the Northern Ireland secretary of state. This left the British government in the position of having alienated both communities.[7]

British forces on the ground were in an invidious position. Sir Alistair Irwin, a platoon commander in the 1970s, and later general officer commanding in Northern Ireland (2000–03), explained: 'The expectation [in 1969] was that the job would be done in a matter of weeks. There was no sense that this was the beginning of a major insurgency that would last a year or two, let alone 35 years.'[8] The British Army's presence exceeded 20,000 personnel in the 1970s, declining steadily to 15,500 in 1998.[9] And although it was scaled down after 1998, *Operation Banner* did not end until 2007.

The logic behind direct rule was to buy time to stem the violence until a more equitable political arrangement could be formulated that involved republicans and unionists.[10] Heath set a strategic direction very early on, announcing that he desired 'reconciliation between Northern Ireland and the Republic of Ireland, reconciliation between Protestants and Catholics, reconciliation between the various political parties in Northern Ireland itself'.[11]

This was far easier said than done. It begged the question as to what kind of political representation to accord to the hardliners. As early as 1972 the Northern Ireland secretary, William Whitelaw, began covert exploratory talks with the IRA. Public exposure of the talks provoked a backlash. It was politically costly for the government to be discovered talking to an armed group that was killing its soldiers. The unionists accused London of selling them out.[12] At this time the political track was entirely exploratory, and provided no evidence to British politicians that it could be relied on. Thus, in the 1970s and 1980s, the dominant facet of British policy remained security measures.

Security forces faced an anti-occupation challenge and a maelstrom of sectarian violence. The IRA targeted British soldiers and the RUC in ambushes and bombings, also assassinating off-duty RUC officers. Unionist paramilitaries, too, carried out 'tit-for-tat' killings, with the UVF and Ulster Defence Association (UDA) targeting IRA members, but also in some instances killing Catholic civilians at random.[13] The RUC expanded to a peak of 13,000 during the Troubles. In 1970 the Ulster Defence Regiment (UDR) was created to provide the RUC with locally recruited military support. But many Catholics suspected the Protestant-dominated RUC and UDR of meting out unfair treatment, and of colluding with UVF and UDA unionist paramilitaries.

Patrolling was a mainstay for British soldiers, with, in Irwin's words, the 'overarching aims of maintaining a high-profile deterrent presence on the ground and gathering intelligence'.[14] Intelligence was vital to the security effort. The IRA envisaged waging a war to reunify Ireland's 32 provinces, but in practice relied on ambushes and terrorism to erode British will.[15] In response, the security forces waged an intelligence-led war to kill the IRA ringleaders. The British Army's 14 Intelligence Company, the Security Service (MI5) and the RUC Special Branch vied to run agents who would betray leading IRA figures. To kill them, the Special Air Service (SAS) was deployed, although alleged SAS complicity in the killing of wrongly targeted civilians led to British debate, during prime minister Margaret Thatcher (1979–90)'s tenure, over how free a rein to allow their operations.[16]

Even when there was no political track to speak of, the British were still in the business of fighting while at least trying to talk. Whitelaw's failed outreach to the IRA emphasised the need for secrecy. In the 1970s, Michael Oatley, a UK Secret Intelligence Service (SIS) officer, opened a covert channel with the IRA. He did so by cultivating contacts with access to the IRA's leadership. Through his agents, Oatley passed messages to the IRA to build confidence and hear its demands. This secret channel helped to bring about prisoner releases and a short-lived ceasefire in 1975. It kept communication lines open during crises such as the 1981 hunger strikes by incarcerated republicans.[17]

British diplomacy also actively supported the effort. The Republic of Ireland would later play a critical role in the peace process. Although motivated by its own interests – the promise of a future republican stake in Stormont, which could forge good links with Dublin, and the promise of reducing violence and criminality along its border, which had resulted in deaths of Irish Garda (police officers) – the British government convinced the taoiseach (Irish prime minister) Garret FitzGerald to sign the 1985 Anglo–Irish Agreement. This sanctioned a role for Dublin as joint broker of a possible future peace agreement in Northern Ireland.

By the close of the 1980s, the Northern Ireland secretary, Peter Brooke, would admit that the IRA could not be defeated militarily, and that talks could follow an end to the violence. In practice, these activities would not follow in successive phases. The UK's conundrum remained unresolved: how to rebalance its strategy so that its political engagement led its security effort, not the other way round.

Politics moves to the foreground but violence continues (1990–1998)

The British government's policy mix was as much a prisoner to events as a shaper of them. Successive British prime ministers saw Northern Ireland as a politically toxic, insoluble issue. Whom to talk to in Northern Ireland to make any progress was a matter of contention. Northern Irish politics did not cease during the Troubles, but the violence greatly disempowered unionist and republican moderates. Moderate parties would later be credited with moving their respective electoral communities to positions of compromise. But they lost out politically in the peace process. The Ulster Unionist Party (UUP) under

David Trimble lost ground to the Democratic Unionist Party (DUP) under hardliner Reverend Ian Paisley, and later Peter Robinson. The Social Democratic and Labour Party (SDLP) under John Hume played an important role in pushing Sinn Féin to reach an agreement, but then lost political ground to it.

Herein is an important truth about London's political approach. Jonathan Powell, chief of staff to prime minister Tony Blair (1997–2007) and lead negotiator in what became the peace process, explained:

> At first we tried to build from the centre, working with the UUP and the SDLP. In the end it was perhaps inevitable that peace could only be made by the DUP and Sinn Féin on the principle … it is only the extremes who can build a durable peace because there is no one left to outflank them.[18]

The British government faced the task of unlocking Northern Ireland's entwined politico-security conundrum. The interrelationship between the armed groups and the hardline politicians was all too apparent to Powell:

> [The IRA] had been the invisible presence at the negotiating table during all our talks. They were the people that Sinn Féin leaders Gerry Adams and Martin McGuinness had needed to persuade to accept difficult compromises, usually going to meet them in an anonymous barn somewhere on the border with the Republic in the night.[19]

Organisationally speaking, Sinn Féin and the IRA were two sides of the same coin. McGuinness and Adams represented a new generation of republican paramilitaries, initially unwilling to negotiate until the British set a date for withdrawal. Their gradual departure from this position relied on the fact that the same leadership body, the Army Council, ran both Sinn Féin and the IRA. This allowed Adams and McGuinness to coordinate political and military strategy in response to British overtures.[20] According to Powell, 'there wasn't a complete overlap in membership and their political imperatives were not the same. Some in the physical force republican movement were not politically subtle and some in Sinn Féin were not engaged in physical violence.'[21]

Powell has described the covert link from London to the IRA as a 'bamboo pipe through which information was passed', and that 'eventually, the link could be used to sustain negotiations'.[22] In 1991, Oatley heard that McGuinness wished to meet him. MI5 now operated the secret channel and in 1993 heard that the IRA wanted a ceasefire. The press became aware of the covert channel that year, just as it was being upgraded to sustain full negotiations and the start of a declared peace process.[23]

It still took years to build trust and reach a breakthrough, as Blair continued the progress John Major (1990–97) had made. There were core issues to resolve: how London would devolve power to Belfast; and how unionists and republicans would share power in Stormont. Before this, the matter of decommissioning IRA arms brought talks to a standstill. Under Major, the UK tried and failed to get the IRA to confirm its 1994 ceasefire as permanent and to decommission its arms. Blair's government resuscitated negotiations. The IRA was told to keep its weapons in sealed dumps for inspection by international observers.[24] British negotiators were softer on decommissioning, but stressed to republicans that they could not expect to dictate the talks with violence, and that the IRA must join the peace process or be excluded. After breaking its ceasefire in 1996, the IRA announced a new ceasefire in 1997.[25]

Ongoing security measures were an essential adjunct to safeguard this progress. With this in mind, restraint was vital in calibrating the security effort. The British government refused to call the Troubles a war, declaring it a law-and-order challenge instead. Soldiers would refrain from patrolling some republican strongholds in South Armagh, where they would almost certainly provoke an armed exchange, and were discouraged from overreacting in the face of provocation.[26] Moreover, the UK's main security aim was to prevent terrorism from destabilising the talks. This entailed a different calculus than a purely security-driven strategy, whereby splintering the IRA by weakening its cohesion may have been understood as a successful outcome. As politics took over, Powell explained that 'Adams and McGuinness were determined to carry the whole movement with them … We did not want to have to make peace lots of times with republican splinter groups.'[27] Thus, preserving republican unity became a British goal.

Adams and McGuinness had to persuade the rank and file of IRA volunteers that the unionists had not been given carte blanche over matters such as decommissioning. Key militants such as Brian Keenan, who ran the IRA bombing campaign on the UK mainland, worked to politicise volunteers and persuade them to end their armed struggle. Not all agreed. Factions splintered to continue the fight.[28] They did so with devastating effect, as in the August 1998 Omagh bombing. The Continuity IRA and the Real IRA became known as 'dissident republicans'; the peace process marginalised these groups, which increasingly fell into a dependency on organised crime both to raise funds and as an end in itself.[29] Grassroots civil-society campaigns, involving citizens who were exhausted by the conflict, would be vital in ostracising further those who continued down the terrorist path.[30]

The British also severed external support to violent republicanism, which had relied on money from sympathetic Irish

Americans and on laundering money in the Republic of Ireland. In the 1970s and 1980s the US had been unwilling to involve itself in Northern Ireland. In the 1990s, Blair enlisted US president Bill Clinton (1993–2001) to support the shutting down of US-based sources of funding, and to endorse the peace process more generally (including the contribution of US mediator George Mitchell). Irish taoiseach Bertie Ahern (1997–2008) stood alongside Major and Blair as joint guarantor of the peace process, granting it a sense of regional balance. And the Garda assisted with border security, shutting down the gun running and money laundering that had enabled the insurgency.

Over the course of the 1990s, the overall security effort was rebalanced to become an enabler of political outreach. For republicans, talks held the promise of a reduced British military presence, the removal of emergency measures (this was referred to as 'normalising security') and, ultimately, of London devolving power to a Stormont and giving republicans a political stake. The negotiations necessitated reassuring unionists that they were not being abandoned. Blair had to emphasise to them that the process was not a slippery slope leading inevitably to a united Ireland.

The pinnacle of this process was the Good Friday Agreement, signed on 10 April 1998. It heralded power-sharing between Sinn Féin and the DUP. The return of devolved power to Northern Ireland was made all the more credible occurring as it did in the same year that the British government devolved power to Welsh and Scottish assemblies. In Northern Ireland, confidence in the security situation would be vital to underpinning confidence in devolution.

The UK's shifting policy mix: securing the peace (1999–2010)
Under the deal, the British Army presence was reduced. Primacy for security was given to MI5 and the Police Service

of Northern Ireland (PSNI), which succeeded the RUC in 2001, bringing Northern Ireland in line with the rest of the UK. MI5 now ran an intelligence fusion centre in Belfast's Loughside army barracks, cohabiting with the PSNI, to facilitate a concerted security effort.[31] As the Northern Ireland chief constable Hugh Orde (2002–09) explained: 'The challenge we face is that we deliver normal policing, but against the background of the terrorist threat. It's very resource intensive.'[32] This included dealing with unionist paramilitaries. In exchange for community projects funded in unionist areas, UDA 'brigade commanders' were told to rein in their volunteers.[33]

As part of the peace process, a peace dividend was offered to both communities if they compromised on power-sharing and ceased violence. The British government admitted to decades of underinvestment in the province – a visit by Gordon Brown in 1998 to announce economic support for Northern Ireland had been the first by a chancellor of the exchequer in nearly 20 years.[34] Economic and political advances in Northern Ireland would take time to consolidate. Building trust in Stormont was laborious, as the DUP and Sinn Féin learned to share power amid a dearth of trust. After years of conflict, politics in Stormont would stall repeatedly.

As slow as progress was, and fragile though it has remained, a milestone was reached on 4 February 2010 as policing and justice powers were devolved from London to Stormont. This had been a core Sinn Féin demand during the talks, and it marked the progress made in the political and security spheres.

The British government had managed a concurrency of approaches to bring about this outcome. While political breakthroughs occurred in the 1990s, coercive security measures remained an important shaper of the climate in which talks took place, but crucially, these security tactics did not try to fracture the republican movement. Rather, the British government sought a viable partner with which to negotiate. This was possible because London had no fundamental opposition to Sinn Féin entering politics, aside from a precondition that the IRA cease its armed struggle. This in turn was only possible due to the ability of Adams and McGuinness to talk to the British and to the IRA volunteers.

Even if British forces did not defeat the IRA, the evidence from both sides suggests that they imposed on the IRA the reality that it could not act with impunity. IRA volunteers admit that informers recruited by the British, and the physical presence of the British Army, reduced the number of attacks they could mount.[35] The result was a gradual containment of the conflict. For Irwin, British forces had 'kept a lid on terrorist activity to allow political activity to take root'.[36]

However, it is important not to impose too much coherency on British strategy, nor to suggest that there was anything like a formal passing of the torch from security to political measures. The convoluted narrative of events suggests that matters did not progress inexorably towards politicising the mainstay of British engagement. Indeed, diplomatic and military practitioners have been at pains to stress just how much events drove their responses.[37] That said, they understood early on the limits of security measures, as Powell reflects: 'After a disastrous start in the 1970s, the British Army had been one of the first participants in Northern Ireland to realise that the campaign could not be won militarily: all they could do was contain the terrorists.'[38] The conundrum was not *whether* to politicise UK government strategy, but *how* to do so.

Clear tensions reside in sending undercover soldiers to kill paramilitaries while also talking to their leadership. The UK's success was in balancing different instruments to the point that its security response became a component of political outreach, ostracising dissident republicans who carried on fighting from politics, and whom the security forces pursued. It was a long and draining process. An insurgency that began in the UK's era of decolonisation would only be subdued in its era of devolution.

Sri Lanka: destroying the LTTE after years of war and talks

The outcome in Sri Lanka completely inverts what happened in Northern Ireland. Sri Lanka eliminated the LTTE with brute force – a victory it achieved in 2009 at huge cost in civilian Tamil lives. Before this, the Sri Lanka Army (SLA) – an overwhelmingly conventional, badly paid and poorly equipped force – had failed to prevent the LTTE from seizing large swathes of territory. Seen in this light, in 2009 the SLA overcame a history of failure. It did so by 'taking advantage of the Tigers' main weaknesses: their hierarchical and conventional structure', as counter-insurgency strategist David Kilcullen has noted, and by 'opposing all external and internal pressure for a ceasefire'.[39] Sri Lanka's government granted the SLA complete freedom to wipe out the LTTE. That the war ended as it did was a catastrophe for the thousands of Tamil civilians killed in the campaign. The conduct of the SLA would be the subject of a subsequent United Nations (UN) investigation:

> [The UN] Panel found credible allegations associated with the final stages of the war. Between September 2008 and 19 May 2009, the Sri Lankan Army advanced its military campaign into Vanni using large-scale and widespread shelling, causing large numbers of civilian deaths ... Tens of thousands lost their lives ... Most civilian casualties in the final phases of the war were caused by government shelling.[40]

That the war would end in such a way was far from preordained. For decades, periods of fighting had been punctuated by negotiations. At first glance, it is easy to dismiss these talks as a historical irrelevance. A different perspective is adopted here. Sri Lanka's government and the LTTE were locked in a long-lasting relationship defined by bloodletting and bargaining. Violence, and the threat of further violence, defined all of their interactions. The government's engagement with the LTTE therefore took place at the intersection between violence and negotiation. As Sri Lankan policy lurched from waging war to talks, it was from the interplay between these efforts that the pendulum eventually came to settle on a brutal, scorched-earth military option.

The onset of insurgency and India's intervention (1983–1990)
For 25 years the LTTE fought the Sri Lankan state. Its aim was to carve out a Tamil homeland from Sinhalese-dominated Sri Lanka. The roots of the war lay in how Sri Lanka had become demarcated along ethnic lines. The largely Buddhist Sinhalese make up roughly three-quarters of Sri Lanka's 20 million people. Their lineage stretches to northern India, whereas Tamil lineage is Dravidian, connecting them to the Tamils of south India. Formerly called Ceylon, Sri Lanka was colonised by the Portuguese, Dutch and British, who governed it as a single administrative unit by amalgamating Tamil and Sinhalese kingdoms.[41] In 1948 Sri Lanka became independent, but Sinhalese subjugation of the minority Tamils followed. Discriminatory legislation, such as the 1956 Sinhala Only Act, restricted use of the Tamil language and impeded employment prospects for Tamils. Whereas Sinhala nationalism had emerged in reaction to colonial domination, Tamil nationalism emerged as a movement for minority rights in the face of Sinhala domination. The two were on a collision course.

Tamil nationalism as a political movement predated the LTTE. In the 1970s the Tamil United Liberation Front (TULF) party polled well in Tamil areas by advocating self-determination. The failure of the TULF to advance its aims paved the way for violent Tamil secessionists. In this, the state was partly to blame. Constitutional amendments in 1983 curtailed freedom of debate on Tamil issues, weakening the TULF's prospects for success. This presaged a militarisation of the cause in the heavily Tamil north and east of the island.[42] The LTTE, founded by Velupillai Prabhakaran, was one of several Tamil armed groups that emerged in this climate. War broke out in July 1983 when the LTTE killed SLA personnel in Jaffna, on Sri Lanka's northern tip. This attack provoked anti-Tamil pogroms in southern Sri Lanka that killed thousands, in turn boosting the insurgency, as Tamil youth flocked to join the LTTE amid a heavy-handed security response.

This first phase of fighting encompassed the Elam War I (1983–87). President J.R. Jayewardene (1978–89) wanted to hold Jaffna, but found that the policy mix was not his to determine. In an overbearing intervention by the prime minister, Indira Gandhi (1966–77, 1980–84), and later her son Rajiv Gandhi (1984–89), India insisted that it broker negotiations between the Sri Lankan government in Colombo and Tamil separatists. These talks took place in Thimpu, Bhutan, in July and August 1985. The Tamil delegation comprised the TULF, LTTE and other Tamil separatist groups active at the time.[43] The government delegation, led by Jayewardene's brother, rejected the demand for total autonomy. The Tamil delegation, as it left the talks, complained of the 'genocidal intent of the Sri Lankan state'.[44] 'Tit-for-tat' violence had paused briefly during the talks but resumed afterwards, starting the pattern of oscillations from fighting to talking that would characterise the conflict.

A full-scale Indian military intervention in Sri Lanka began in 1987. India's impulse to intervene was driven by its proximity, just 30 kilometres away, its own potentially restive Tamil population in the southern Indian state of Tamil Nadu, and, above all else, a desire to exploit Sri Lanka's civil war to boost its own regional standing. India's ill-conceived strategy was to escalate the war, and then to step in to broker its end. Between 1983 and 1987, India's military trained thousands of Tamil refugees to fight the SLA as a pretext for its intervention.[45] In July 1987 Rajiv Gandhi flew to Colombo to sign an accord with Jayewardene that codified India's role in ending the war, and 80,000 Indian peacekeepers were deployed to oversee implementation of the Indo-Sri Lankan peace accord.

Sri Lanka's government could do little but acquiesce. Colombo was in no position to block India's deployment. Sri Lankan security forces were distracted at this time by a Marxist insurrection in the south of the island, which it brutally suppressed through killings and mass imprisonments.[46] In northern Sri Lanka, the LTTE, which had not been consulted as part of the peace accord, fought Indian soldiers who attempted to forcibly disarm it. Political opinion in Colombo became increasingly livid at India's exertion of power at the expense of Sri Lankan sovereignty. President Ranasinghe Premadasa (1989–93), who had replaced Jayewardene, even secretly colluded with the LTTE to force the Indians out. As India's military losses crossed the 1,000 mark it chose to withdraw its forces in March 1990. In May the following year an LTTE suicide bomber assassinated Rajiv Gandhi as he campaigned for re-election in Tamil Nadu.

Premadasa had secured his primary aim: India's exit from Sri Lanka. He had done so through dialogue with the LTTE, which lasted into 1990 but collapsed after India's withdrawal removed their common foe. The Sri Lankan government may have restored control over its own policies. But could it advance its strategic aims in relation to an ascendant LTTE?

Sri Lanka tries – and fails – to use war to dictate peace terms (1991–2001)

The commitment of either side to a genuine political settlement and to move away from maximalist demands was questionable. In the 1990s the LTTE came to monopolise the Tamil nationalist podium. It killed TULF leaders and eclipsed all rival groups with Prabhakaran's cultish leadership. Its tactics were a brutal mix of guerrilla war, conventional war, terror and assassination. An LTTE suicide bomber killed Premadasa in May 1993. In Sri Lanka's north and east the LTTE had founded a proto-state called Tamil Eelam ('homeland'), replete with its own administrative structures.[47] Even at the apex of its power, however, the LTTE failed to develop a truly political facet. In 2001 moderates formed the Tamil National Alliance party, but it duly recognised the LTTE as the only entity able to negotiate on behalf of Tamils.[48] The LTTE came to see itself as the government-in-waiting of a Tamil state.[49]

The Tamil uprising clearly had political roots, but Colombo struggled to come to a consensus over the political dimensions of Sri Lanka's response. Talks with the LTTE became hostage to Sri Lanka's system of proportional representation. Its political parties failed to produce a government consensus over the desirability of a deal with the LTTE.[50] Colombo's motivation for talks was also driven by its varying battlefield fortunes. Unequivocal defeat of the LTTE was well beyond the SLA's grasp for decades. As the island became divided into two spheres of influence, the war became a positional conflict with relatively clear lines of demarcation, but the SLA struggled to make any gains. This pushed the government to pursue talks as an opportunity for its forces to recuperate.[51]

Nevertheless, in the mid-1990s the president, Chandrika Kumaratunga (1994–2005), tried to inflict battlefield reverses on the LTTE to force the Tamils to accept her proposals for a settlement. In 1994 she began talks with the LTTE, and the following year floated a devolution proposal. A ceasefire was agreed in January 1995, but hardline Sinhalese parties diluted the substance of her proposal, and the LTTE pulled out of talks in April, complaining that the state was not taking its demands seriously. The Elam Wars II (1990–95) and III (1995–2002) over-lapped with these talks. Sri Lanka had tried and failed to use its military position to improve its bargaining position and dictate the peace. Instead, the LTTE had the greater fighting momentum, even staging a brazen assault on aeroplanes parked at Colombo airport in July 2001.

From Norway's failed mediation to the LTTE's annihilation (2002–2009)

Sinhalese hardliners had always tried to portray Tamil agitation for greater political rights as 'terrorism'. This conflation helped to mobilise Sinhala support for the government's security policies and delegitimise the Tamil nationalist cause, in all of its facets. And Sri Lankan diplomacy worked to stymie any international validation of the LTTE's claim to a Tamil home-land. The LTTE was proscribed by the European Union (EU) and US as a terrorist entity and, after 9/11, Sri Lanka could make the case that it was waging its own war on terrorism.

Despite this, yet another external intervention rebalanced the Sri Lankan state's policy mix. With the consent of both sides, Norway – a major Sri Lankan aid donor – was invited to be an honest broker of talks.[52] Norway helped to mediate a cease-fire in February 2002, the terms of which left the Sri Lankan state in control of Tamil cities such as Trincomalee, Batticaloa and Jaffna, but left the LTTE in control of rural areas under its sway.[53] The prime minister, Ranil Wickremesinghe (2001–04), lifted a ban on the LTTE to allow it to participate in talks, several rounds of which occurred in Oslo, Berlin and Bangkok.[54]

The LTTE approached the talks with maximalist demands, insisting that the government grant it the authority to autonomously govern areas it controlled. While LTTE negotiator Anton Balasingham presented an erudite front, away from the talks, Prabhakaran's authority remained absolute, as did his ability to resume the fighting.[55] The talks also failed because each side had such mixed motives. After 9/11, while the LTTE was keen to show its political viability, it may have never genuinely countenanced demobilisation or power-sharing.[56] A need for breathing space also underpinned Colombo's motivation, Wickremesinghe hoping that a pause in the fighting might reinvigorate Sri Lanka's economy.[57]

By late 2003, not only were the talks stalling, but they had plunged Colombo into political infighting. The Sri Lankan ministers leading the talks were fired. Wickremesinghe was blamed by president Kumaratunga for being too lenient with the LTTE. Kumaratunga, in turn, was under pressure from Sinhalese nationalists in the Janatha Vimukthi Peramuna party, who bitterly opposed any concessions to the LTTE, leading her to suspend parliament.[58] So keen were the hardliners to de-legitimise the LTTE that, even after a tsunami in December 2004 killed and displaced tens of thousands of Sri Lankans, the government constrained the aid flow to LTTE-run areas so as not to empower it.

In 2005, Mahinda Rajapaksa (2005–15) defeated Wickremesinghe in the presidential election and government strategy towards the LTTE switched focus. A further round of talks occurred in Geneva in 2006, but the process by now was moribund. The SLA was being readied to resume – and escalate – the war. Sri Lanka's hardliners used the final phase of talks to begin to prepare for a military victory for which they had never ceased yearning.[59]

Rajapaksa de-linked the use of force from negotiations. The seeds of this strategy were planted as the Norwegian-mediated talks came to an end. The 2004 defection of LTTE commander 'Colonel Karuna' (a *nom de guerre*) and those under his command weakened Prabhakaran. Karuna's forces colluded with the SLA to fight the LTTE.[60] The SLA also underwent rearmament and modernisation, procuring Chinese and Pakistani weapons, under General Sarath Fonseka and Rajapaksa's brother the defence secretary, Gotabaya Rajapaksa. Those favouring a resumption of the war now dominated key Sri Lankan ministries.[61]

The Eelam War IV began in 2006. The SLA used better tactics than in the past, such as commando attacks behind LTTE lines, but its overall approach remained bluntly conventional. Facing concentrations of Tamil civilians who were being used by the LTTE as human shields, the SLA bombed these areas. According to a UN official based in Sri Lanka at the time, the SLA fired 'warning bombardments' to spur civilians to flee, and their failure to do so was enough to determine complicity with the LTTE.[62] A subsequent UN investigation found that indiscriminate artillery fire caused between 10,000 and 40,000 civilian deaths.[63] Amid these relentless attacks the LTTE suffered heavy losses, and given Sri Lanka's island geography they had no avenues for escape once cornered. On 19 May 2009, Prabhakaran was found dead on the battlefield, a symbolic moment amidst the end to the campaign.

The war had involved considerable brutality on both sides. The LTTE did not shirk from using suicide bombers, recruiting child soldiers and assassinating officials. The LTTE had also massacred civilians to consolidate its hold over territory, including many Sri Lankan Muslims.[64] While this does not excuse the bluntness of the 2009 campaign, it explains why the SLA moved so decisively to secure a goal that had eluded it for so long. Under Rajapaksa and Fonseka, the SLA had prioritised destroying the LTTE over any consideration of *jus in bello* and the proportionality of violence.

The government gave the SLA full operational freedom. No ceasefires were granted, so the LTTE could not use them to regroup as it had in the past. The government embarked on a series of supporting activities to ensure its strategy would work. Staving off international pressure for a ceasefire was crucial. A Rajapaksa official told an Indian publication that 'we didn't want the international community to force peace nego-tiations on us'.[65] Although Western countries condemned the 2009 SLA offensive, Sri Lanka escaped with only their censure. And China provided Sri Lanka with diplomatic cover, based on a friendship from which China gained maritime rights around Sri Lanka. This was the political approach accompanying the final SLA offensive.

That the war was ended by brute force does not lessen the importance of grasping how, for many years, Sri Lanka used coercion and dialogue. Sri Lankan hardliners may have remained fixated on defeating the LTTE, but the state did not use relentless violence throughout. In the mid-1990s it tried to exploit its battlefield gains at the negotiating table, but failed to concurrently advance its military and political positions. Ultimately, the oscillating emphasis between fighting and talking bought Rajapaksa time to set up a militarised endgame.

The question remains as to what status Tamils will now have in Sri Lanka.

Rajapaksa traded off post-war triumphalism to consolidate his political base, and was slow to introduce a meaningful reconciliation process, or amendments to how Tamil areas would be governed. The SLA may have destroyed the LTTE, but the task of addressing the underlying political currents that gave rise to the insurrection in the first place would be another matter.

Delivering a decisive outcome against armed groups

There is neither a 'Northern Ireland option' nor a 'Sri Lanka option' for victory. There will seldom be a straightforward path towards a decisive outcome – only a meandering road that often leads to dead ends. This is especially true if states get off to a bad start, being caught by surprise at the outbreak of an insurgency, and overreacting in a way that exacerbates the conflict. Successive governments may well inherit a deteriorating situation from their forebears. Whether they aspire to become peacemakers, or to be lauded for their military prowess, seldom will they rely on just one response. Just as war can have a part to play in securing peace, attempted dialogue may well presage military victory. And this combination may well arise more by accident than by design. Although the Sri Lankan government ultimately achieved a violent outcome, its strategy was not exclusively a violent one. Although the British government achieved political accommodation, its strategy was not purely ameliorative.

There are costs associated with securing a genuinely decisive outcome. As Sri Lanka shows, eradicating an armed group root and branch can be a cruel affair. As Northern Ireland shows, armed groups are violent, illegal entities that may have to be legitimised so that a peace process can take place. And if negotiations are to make progress, addressing the grievances underlying an insurgency may ultimately involve political reform, such as the UK enacted towards Northern Ireland within the wider process of devolution.

Notes

1 Tony Blair, speech in Belfast, Northern Ireland, *Guardian*, 17 October 2002, http://www.theguardian.com/politics/2002/oct/17/northernireland.devolution.

2 Mahinda Rajapaksa, speech at the opening of parliament, 19 May 2009, http://www.satp.org.

3 John Bew, 'Collective Amnesia and the Northern Ireland Model of Conflict Resolution', *The Lessons of Northern Ireland* (London School of Economics, IDEAS Special Edition, 2011), p. 19.

4 Paul Dixon, 'Guns First, Talks Later: Neoconservatives and the Northern Ireland Peace Process', *The Journal of Imperial and Commonwealth History*, vol. 39, no. 4, 2011, pp. 649–76.

5 Paul Bew, *Ireland: The Politics of Enmity 1789–2006* (Oxford: Oxford University Press, 2007), pp. 416–23, 460–1, 446–8, 570.

6 *Ibid.*, pp. 495–7, 503.

7 *Ibid.*, pp. 508–9.

8 Sir Alistair Irwin, 'The Military Response', in James Dingley (ed.), *Combating Terrorism in Northern Ireland* (Abingdon: Routledge, 2009), p. 213.

9 Neil Southern, 'The Royal Ulster Constabulary and the Terrorism threat', in Dingley (ed.), *Combating Terrorism in Northern Ireland*, p. 179; Irwin, 'The Military Response', p. 200.

10 Peter Neumann, *Britain's Long War* (Basingstoke: Palgrave Macmillan, 2003), pp. 70–1.

11 Edward Heath speech in Blackpool, 13 October 1973, http://www.britishpoliticalspeech.org/speech-archive.htm?speech=120.

12 Andrew Mumford, 'Covert Peacemaking: Clandestine Negotiations and Backchannels with the Provisional IRA during the Early "Troubles", 1972–76', *The Journal of Imperial and Commonwealth History*, vol. 39, no. 4, 2011, pp. 633–48.

13 Peter Neumann, 'Rise of the Paramilitaries', in Dingley (ed.), *Combating Terrorism in Northern Ireland*, pp. 44–5.

14 Irwin, 'The Military Response', p. 208.

15 M.L.R. Smith, *Fighting For Ireland: The Military Strategy of the Republican Movement* (London: Routledge, 1997).

16 Christopher Andrew, *Defence of the Realm: The Authorized History of MI5* (London: Allen Lane, 2009), pp. 619–26; Mark Urban, *Big Boys' Rules: The SAS and the Secret Struggle Against the IRA* (London: Faber & Faber, 1992), p. 211.

17 Peter Taylor, *Brits: The War Against the IRA* (London: Bloomsbury Publishing, 2001), pp. 163–81; Jonathan Powell, *Great Hatred, Little Room: Making Peace in Northern Ireland* (London: Bodley Head, 2009), pp. 66–70.

18 Powell, *Great Hatred, Little Room*, p. 312.

19 *Ibid.*, p. 2.

20 Anthony Richards, 'Terrorist Groups and their Political Fronts', in Dingley (ed.), *Combating Terrorism in Northern Ireland*, pp. 80–1, 88; Bew, *Politics of Enmity*, p. 524.

21 Powell, *Great Hatred, Little Room*, p. 124.

22 *Ibid.*, pp. 71–3. McGuinness later denied sending the message to defend himself against hardliners.

23 Taylor, *Brits*, pp. 163–81; Powell, *Great Hatred, Little Room*, pp. 66–73.

24 'Timeline: Northern Ireland's Road to Peace', last updated 27 January 2006, http://news.bbc.co.uk/1/hi/northern_ireland/4072261.stm.

25 Powell, *Great Hatred, Little Room*, pp. 11–14, 147, 176, 318.

26 Urban, *Big Boys' Rules*, pp. 69–73, 81, 161–4; Frank Ledwidge, *Losing Small Wars* (New Haven, CT: Yale University Press, 2011), pp. 184–5.

27 Powell, *Great Hatred, Little Room*, p. 25.

28 *Ibid.*, pp. 160–79; Rogelio Alonso, *The IRA and Armed Struggle* (London New York: Routledge, 2003), pp. 138–68.

29 Margaret Gilmore, 'No Way Back? Examining the Background and Response to the Rise of Dissident Terrorist Activity in Northern Ireland', *RUSI Journal*, vol. 154, no. 2, April 2009, pp. 50–5; Neumann, 'Rise of the Paramilitaries', p. 44.

30 Brian Gormally, 'From Punishment Violence to Restorative Justice in Northern Ireland', in Sophie Haspeslagh and Zahbia Yousuf (eds), *Local Engagement with Armed Groups in the Midst of Violence* (London: Conciliation Resources, 2015), pp. 27–9.

31 Gilmore, 'No Way Back?', pp. 53–4.

32 *Ibid.*, pp. 50–5.

33 Powell, *Great Hatred, Little Room*, p. 226.

34 *Ibid.*, p. 115; Neumann, *Britain's Long War* charts the evolution of British economic engagement in Northern Ireland: pp. 35–8, 65–7, 92–6, 117–20, 141–5, 174–6.

35 Alonso, *Armed Struggle*, p. 161; Urban, *Big Boys' Rules*, pp. 169, 238–41.

36 Irwin, 'The Military Response', p. 215.

37 *Ibid.*, pp. 223–4.

38 Powell, *Great Hatred, Little Room*, p. 310; Andrew, *Defence of the Realm*, p. 620.

39 David Kilcullen, 'The Global Context of Counterterrorism: Strategy, Ethics, and Sustainability in Sri Lanka's COIN Experience', address to 'Defeating Terrorism, The Sri Lankan Experience', Colombo, 1 June 2011, http://groundviews.org/2011/06/01/the-global-context-of-counterterrorism-strategy-ethics-and-sustainability-in-sri-lanka%E2%80%99s-coin-experience/.

40 'Report of the Secretary-General's Panel of Experts on Accountability in Sri Lanka', UN, 31 March 2011, p. ii, http://www.un.org/News/dh/infocus/Sri_Lanka/POE_Report_Full.pdf.

41 Deidre McConnell, 'The Tamil People's Right to Self-Determination', *Cambridge Review of International Affairs*, vol. 21, no. 1, March 2008, pp. 59–76; 'Sri Lanka at the Cross-Roads of History' conference, Centre for Research in Arts, Social Sciences and Humanities, Cambridge University, 3–4 June 2011.

42 Suthaharan Nadarajah and Dhananjayan Sriskandarajah, 'Liberation Struggle or Terrorism? The Politics of Naming the LTTE', *Third World Quarterly*, vol. 26, no. 1, 2005, pp. 87–100.

43 Gordon Weiss, *The Cage: The Fight for Sri Lanka and the Last Days of the Tamil Tigers* (London: Bodley Head, 2011), pp. 81–2. At this point, the LTTE was one of several Tamil militant groups alongside

the Eelam People's Revolutionary Liberation Front, the Tamil Eelam Liberation Organization and the Eelam Revolutionary Organisation of Students.

44 S. Sivanayagam, 'The Thimpu Talks 1985: Sinhala–Tamil Conflict and the Indian Factor', http:// tamilnation.co/conflictresolution/ t a m i l e e l a m / 8 5 t h i m p u / sivanayagam.pdf.

45 International Crisis Group, 'India and Sri Lanka after the LTTE' (Asia Report 206, 23 June 2011), pp. 2–4 for a discussion of the Indian peacekeeping force.

46 The JVP was a Marxist movement discontented with the dominant Sinhalese regime. After its military defeat the JVP turned away from insurrection to politics, and became a strident political opponent of Tamil self-determination.

47 International Crisis Group, 'Sri Lanka: Sinhala Nationalism and the Elusive Southern Consensus' (Asia Report 141, 7 November 2007), pp. 1, 5, 15–18.

48 International Crisis Group 'Sri Lanka: The Failure of the Peace Process' (Asia Report 124, 28 November 2006), pp. 12–13.

49 Suthaharan Nadarajah and Luxshi Vimalarajah, *The Politics of Transformation: The LTTE and the 2002–2006 Peace Process in Sri Lanka* (Berghof Transitions Series 4, Berghof Research Center for Constructive Conflict Management 2008), pp. 28–31.

50 Chandra Lekha Sriram, *Peace as Governance: Power-Sharing, Armed Groups and Contemporary Peace Negotiations* (London: Palgrave, 2008); International Crisis Group,

'Sri Lanka: The failure of the peace process', p. 14.

51 Sriram, *Peace as Governance*, chapter 3: 'Sri Lanka: The Repeated Failures of Inclusion Incentives', p. 75; International Crisis Group, 'Sri Lanka: The Failure of the Peace Process', p. 14.

52 Nadarajah and Vimalarajah, *The Politics of Transformation*, p. 36; International Crisis Group, 'Sri Lanka: The Failure of the Peace Process', p. 5.

53 International Crisis Group, 'Sri Lanka: The Failure of the Peace Process', p. 5.

54 Nadarajah and Vimalarajah, *The Politics of Transformation*, p. 95.

55 International Crisis Group, 'Sri Lanka: The Failure of the Peace Process'.

56 Nadarajah and Vimalarajah, *The Politics of Transformation*, pp. 36, 44.

57 Sriram, *Peace as Governance*, pp. 82, 85, 101, 105; International Crisis Group, 'Sri Lanka: The Failure of the Peace Process', p. 5.

58 International Crisis Group, 'Sri Lanka: Sinhala Nationalism', p. 13.

59 International Crisis Group, 'Sri Lanka: The Failure of the Peace Process', pp. 10–11.

60 Sriram, *Peace as Governance*, pp. 89–90.

61 Weiss, *The Cage,* pp. 93, 248.

62 *Ibid.*, pp. 133–4.

63 'Report of the Secretary-General's Panel of Experts on Accountability in Sri Lanka', p. 41, para. 137.

64 See 'The Costs of War' in International Crisis Group, 'Sri Lanka's Return to War: Limiting the Damage' (Asia Report 146, 20 February 2008), p. 9.

65 'The Sri Lanka Option: Friends Like These', *The Economist,* 22 May 2010.

CHAPTER TWO

Struggling to move from military stalemate to negotiations

A mutually hurting stalemate defines the moment as ripe for resolution: both sides are locked in a situation from which they cannot escalate the conflict ... [However], the asymmetry of internal conflict rarely produces the stalemate needed for negotiation.

William Zartman[1]

Negotiation is undertaken for the dual purpose of gaining time to buttress a position (military, political, social, economic) and to wear down, frustrate, and harass the opponent. Few, if any, essential concessions are to be expected from the revolutionary side.

Mao Zedong[2]

In failing to secure a decisive outcome, states can get stuck along the way. This chapter looks at two conflicts that, for decades, have fallen short of being either militarily or politically decisive. Turkey's war with the Kurdistan Workers' Party (PKK) began in 1984, but a comprehensive military victory has proved as elusive as a negotiated end – both of which

Turkey has tried for at different times. Colombia's war with the Revolutionary Armed Forces of Colombia (FARC), which began in 1964, has lasted even longer and its strategy has oscillated between quests for a deal and military offensives.

Civil–military tensions have hampered the unity of purpose with which Colombia and Turkey have been able to act. For reasons that are unique to the histories of each country, generals were able to impose their will on politicians at important moments in each conflict. This hampered both states from being able to accept the trade-offs between their political and military approaches, leading to attempts to pursue both objectives, and the failure to achieve either.

Missed opportunities abound in the long histories of these conflicts. As William Zartman is quoted above as observing, a military deadlock may well be necessary to create an opening for talks, but may not be sufficient to produce a deal. Many variables must fall into place for a viable negotiation process to begin, including sufficient will from all sides, the impact of spoilers being minimised and neighbouring states helping to guarantee a settlement. And, as Mao alludes to in the quotation above, all the while, an armed group may be talking simply to play for time.

Colombia: five decades of tilting between fighting and talking

Why has the Colombian state been unable to end its war with FARC for so long? FARC formed with the aim of overthrowing the government on behalf of the rural poor. It grew from just dozens of members in the 1960s to an estimated 18,000 in the early 2000s, at the peak of its strength.[3] In that time FARC not only became a major military force, but also deeply entrenched itself in the socio-economic life of the country and its drug trade, leading the group to drift far away from its ideological moorings. Accordingly, FARC is a complicated movement that has demanded a multifaceted response from the state.

Successive Colombian governments have wrestled with the conundrum of balancing the various strands of their responses. Policy formulation in Bogotá has fallen victim to civil–military tensions, as Colombia's politicians have at times felt undermined by their generals, and vice versa. Colombia's strategy has periodically lurched from fighting FARC in its jungle strongholds, to trying to secure its demilitarisation through negotiations. And the Colombian state has at times fallen into practices that have exacerbated the war, such as backing right-wing paramilitary groups to fight on its behalf.

So often has its approach oscillated between fighting and talking, the very fact of these oscillations gives some substance to an understanding of Colombia's strategy. The periodic swing of the pendulum between approaches is especially important to grasp in the context of the extended time frame involved. In late 2012, as Colombian negotiators began talking to FARC in Havana, Cuba, the question centred on whether this time things would be different. Unlike in previous failed peace overtures, President Juan Manuel Santos (2010–) would argue that he has not only the political will to see talks through, but also sufficient military pressure to push FARC into a position from which a negotiated settlement is more likely to be secured. It is a claim that highlights the difficulties of moving from a military stalemate to negotiations. On this theme, an abundance of useful insights are littered throughout Colombia's historical record in managing FARC.

The roots of Colombia's left-wing armed groups (1964–1981)

FARC's armed struggle has deep roots in left-wing ideologies. Inequitable resource distribution and the subjugation of peasant labour by landowners has left many Colombians feeling dispossessed.[4] These were the currents of discontent that gave rise to the Colombian Communist Party (PCC) in 1930. The PCC weathered the storm of *La Violencia* (1948–58), a period during which more than 200,000 people died in a civil war for control of Colombia's agricultural land. It was fought between paramilitaries linked to the Colombian Conservative Party and Colombian Liberal Party. To bring this bitter war to an end, a bipartisan political system was established, and the paramilitaries demobilised.

After *La Violencia*, PCC members founded FARC as the party's armed wing. The PCC had already set up peasant self-defence groups, but they faced army harassment. FARC combined the PCC tradition of grassroots peasant networks with the guerrilla tactics of former Liberal Party-linked paramilitaries. Led by Manuel Marulanda Vélez, FARC built its reputation as the defender of peasant interests. To defend their own interests, landowners set up right-wing paramilitary groups, which received the backing of Colombia's military to fight FARC on behalf of the state. As the country's drug trade became a focal point of the struggle, FARC's left-wing credentials became ever more diluted.[5]

While FARC is the longest-lasting and largest left-wing armed group that Colombia has seen, it has not been the only one. The National Liberation Army (ELN), formed in 1965 by a Cuban revolution-inspired student group, still exists. Also of relevance are a host of smaller groups that the Colombian government succeeded in demobilising in the 1990s. They include: the Popular Liberation Army (EPL), which splintered from FARC in 1969; M19, formed in 1974 by urban radicals; the Workers Revolutionary Party (PRT), founded in 1982; and the Quintin Lame Armed Movement (MAQL), a guerrilla group of indigenous peoples founded in 1984.[6] Negotiations involving these groups will be discussed below, primarily for the precedent they have set in how FARC has been handled. FARC, too, was a relatively marginal group until the 1980s, when it substantially expanded its size and presence across Colombia, cutting its ties to the PCC and seeking to become a national movement in its own right.[7]

Colombia's shifting emphasis between fighting and talking (1982–2002)

Over the course of several decades the nature of Colombia's conflict has changed. The character of FARC's insurgency has evolved, as has the standing of Colombia's other left- and right-wing armed groups, and the wider regional climate in which they have operated. So too has the political environment in Bogotá, as factors influencing government responses to FARC have changed, sometimes beyond recognition. Thus, the passage of time is a critical factor in grasping Colombia's periodically shifting policy mix.

Dealing with FARC is an undertaking that has spanned generations of Colombian politicians, soldiers and civil servants. No Colombian government has ever been able to completely ignore what has come before. After a particular combination of policies had been attempted, subsequent governments would inherit the legacy of its outcomes. FARC proved to be too deeply entrenched to be defeated militarily. Consequently, the choice of strategy has never been a binary one between fighting and talking, even if the political will in Bogotá has at times favoured one approach over the other. It is the sequencing and balancing of approaches that has reflected Colombia's strategic calculus.

President Belisario Betancur (1982–86) prioritised negotiations with the guerrilla groups. The government signed ceasefires with FARC, M19 and EPL in 1984. But security operations persisted, notably after M19 brazenly launched attacks in Bogotá in 1985 and killed some of Colombia's supreme court judges. In contrast, FARC maintained its ceasefire, responding positively to Betancur's political overtures by forming Patriotic Union (UP), a political party, in 1985. This attempt to politicise its standing ended badly: UP was brutally wiped out by right-wing paramilitaries and the army, who also killed the UP presidential candidate a year after he had contested Colombia's 1986 election Thereafter, FARC approached offers of negotiation warily. Rather than seeking to become a political actor, FARC would look instead to its military strength to guarantee its stature.[8] Although both sides were responsible for the resumption of violence, the Colombian military had notably defied Betancur's ceasefire order. With security responses masterminded by the military, and negotiations favoured by politicians, these approaches could mutually undermine each other.[9]

President Virgilio Barco (1986–90) tried to avoid this fate by gaining military support for his peace overtures. Barco made little progress talking to FARC, which ended its ceasefire in 1987. But he and his successor César Gaviria (1990–94) secured deals with M19, EPL, PRT and MAQL. Some 4,000 guerrillas turned in their arms to an international verification mission.[10] In return, the demobilised guerrillas were allowed to form political parties. Former M19 members contested the 1990 elections, but the party later faded from the political scene. Moreover, right-wing paramilitaries continued to kill former guerrillas. FARC and ELN – the armed groups remaining 'at large' – understandably concluded that demobilisation would at best bring mixed results, and at worst could lead to their deaths.[11]

The state derived its own lessons: that armed groups would not seriously countenance demobilisation unless sufficiently pressured, militarily, beforehand. As Professor Carlo Nasi has written, 'the preferred scenario for the Colombian establishment would be to negotiate with (and not make any concessions to) virtually defeated rebel groups'.[12] However, achieving such military successes against FARC proved difficult. During Gaviria's tenure, the military attacked FARC headquarters in Casa Verde in 1990. President Ernesto Samper (1994–98) continued the security response. In 1997 the army launched operations against FARC in the areas of Meta, Caquetá and Huila. But right-wing paramilitaries retained the greatest power to hurt FARC and ELN. In the same year several paramilitary groups combined to form the United Self-Defense Forces of Colombia (AUC). With army support, and with money from the drug trade, the AUC assassinated many FARC and ELN members.[13]

President Andrés Pastrana (1998–2002) brought negotiations to the fore of his strategy. As president-elect he had met the FARC leadership, hearing their demands that the AUC be reined in and for the creation of a demilitarised zone in which FARC would not be targeted, which Pastrana created once in power. But the generals criticised Pastrana for appeasing FARC. They feared that FARC was using the demilitarised zone to consolidate its strength and deepen its profits from the drug trade. The AUC stepped in, presenting itself as a bulwark against Pastrana's capitulation, and escalating its attacks. As a result, FARC suffered extrajudicial killings even as it was talking with the Pastrana government. FARC responded by assassinating high-profile state officials, and reverted to seeing these talks as a component of its armed struggle, rather than seriously countenancing disarmament as an option.[14]

Nevertheless, lessons emerged from Pastrana's failed talks. FARC had insisted that the talks had to address Colombia's underlying socio-economic issues. An unwieldy 47-point negotiation agenda was agreed on, but this proved far too broad. In contrast, Barco and Gaviria had pursued very narrow negotiation agendas with M19, EPL, PRT and MAQL, offering concessions in exchange for demobilisation. Such a transactional focus was not possible with FARC, which, due to its size and strong military position, could influence the terms of the talks.[15] Ultimately, the talks collapsed and in 2002 the army reoccupied the demilitarised zone as FARC withdrew to resume its war.

This has been an often repeated problem for Colombia, with negotiations undone by reciprocal violence.[16] Absolute security during talks could never be guaranteed, of course. In such a geographically dispersed, long-standing and bitter conflict, some clashes would always be likely to persist. But more effective coordination between Colombia's security and political tracks would be essential if the cycle of failure was ever to be broken.

Fighting FARC before the start of the Havana talks (2002–2014)

President Alvaro Uribe (2002–10) sought a military victory over FARC. No doubt as a reaction to Pastrana's failed talks, Uribe tipped the strategic seesaw towards force. He presided over a military surge and operations in 2002–03 to dislodge FARC from areas surrounding Bogotá. *Plan Patriota*, launched in 2004, aimed to achieve the same in the south, and pushed FARC into something of a retreat.[17] These operations were one prong of Uribe's strategy. Meanwhile, a counter-narcotics policy that had US backing constricted FARC profits from the drug trade. Moreover, the AUC was abolished. This was followed by a demobilisation programme for the right-wing paramilitaries. However, rates of recidivism were high, as ex-AUC paramilitaries joined powerful criminal groups such as Los Urabeños, which carried on AUC-like activities in all but name, including killing FARC and ELN members.[18]

According to Uribe's strategy, negotiations would be deferred until FARC had been sufficiently weakened. Rather than pursue talks and security operations simultaneously, as his predecessors had done, Uribe wanted to exert as much military pressure as possible before taking a political approach.[19] Not everyone was as patient in waiting for talks. Venezuelan president Hugo Chávez (1999–2013) offered to mediate between Bogotá and FARC, but these talks never got off the ground due to Uribe's focus on fighting FARC and his opposition to Chávez's involvement.[20]

Santos took office in 2010 and again reordered Colombia's approach. His primary goal was a negotiated settlement with FARC, and one on which he staked his personal political reputation. Ongoing security operations kept pressure on FARC, but they were now weighed up against political overtures. Santos was well placed to build on the momentum of Uribe's military surge, having served as Uribe's defence minister (2006–09). The early period of his presidency was therefore more a continuation of trends in the security response than a clear break.

One such trend was close Colombian cooperation with US security agencies. The US war on drugs had persisted for years, with Colombia receiving US support against guerrillas and drugs traffickers. US involvement gained new impetus after 9/11. US president George W. Bush (2001–09) authorised the US military to counter FARC as a part of the global war on terror. In 2002, US Southern Command (SOUTHCOM), which was responsible for all US military activities in Central and South America, was given additional authority and resources to assist Colombian security forces. US military aid to Colombia increased sharply in a short space of time, from US$225 million in 2001, to US$680m in 2004.[21] While US forces were not permitted to fight FARC, US intelligence helped to reduce the time between locating FARC fighters and Colombian security forces being dispatched to attack them.[22]

Another trend spanning the Uribe and Santos eras was the targeting of FARC leaders. In March 2008 Colombian soldiers crossed the border into Ecuador, killing FARC deputy commander Raúl Reyes. Tensions escalated with Ecuador and with Venezuela, where FARC also had a presence. Later in 2008 two more leaders of the FARC secretariat died: Iván Rios was killed by a bodyguard and Manuel Marulanda died of natural causes. FARC named Alfonso Cano as its new leader. In November 2011 Colombian security forces killed Cano in southwest Colombia. In total, 16 FARC leaders were killed during Uribe's tenure, and 47 more under Santos (as of December 2013, just over a year into the Havana talks).[23] According to government figures, in the two years preceding September 2013, security forces killed, captured or demobilised 5,374 FARC and ELN fighters. The accumulated impact of these security gains would be trumpeted by the state: according to official statistics, in 2000 half of Colombia's 1,100 municipalities suffered violence from armed groups; by 2012, only 11% of municipalities were thus afflicted.[24]

Unfolding in parallel were secret preparatory talks with FARC, paving the way for negotiations to begin in Havana in late 2012. A five-point negotiation agenda was announced in October 2012. Santos stated that only agreement on all five points would permit a deal to be reached. During 2013 agreement was reached on two points (rural development and the participation of former FARC members in politics). The 2014 presidential election turned into something of a referendum on the peace process, and Santos was re-elected, capitalising on a civic peace movement that reflected the exhaustion of so many of Colombia's citizens who wanted an end to the conflict. According to Colombia's National Centre for Historical Memory, an estimated 220,000 people had been killed in the conflict by 2013, the majority of whom were civilians.[25] So great has the suffering been that a strain of public and political opinion has demanded that FARC leaders face justice, leaving the negotiators in Havana with a careful balancing act to secure a deal.

Crucially, the talks in Havana did not spell a suspension in security operations. Santos made clear from the outset that there would be no ceasefire until the talks were completed, to prevent FARC from using the talks as a respite from the fighting.[26] Ensuring military restraint in the face of ongoing provocations by FARC was a concern. In early 2014 Santos removed the armed forces chief of staff, General Leonardo Barrero, after he resisted investigations into so-called 'false positives' – military personnel who had claimed that dead civilians belonged to FARC to inflate body-count statistics. His replacement, General Pablo Rodríguez, was a veteran of anti-FARC operations, but perhaps more crucially said that 'it is the work of soldiers that has brought us closer to peace'.[27] Bombings and ambushes were still occasional occurrences, because some FARC units were keen to spoil the talks and demonstrate their standing.

A deal with FARC would not bring an end to Colombia's security woes. FARC has become ever more closely entwined with criminal and trafficking gangs, against which the state has mobilised a police and judicial response.[28] However, a deal would nevertheless be a milestone in government efforts to improve security. In the longer run, for a deal to be implemented, concurrent security measures would be required to ensure trust and to deal with spoilers, whether from rejectionist FARC splinter groups or right-wing paramilitaries.

The Havana talks are a useful vantage point from which to take stock of five decades of Colombia's 'fight–talk/talk–fight' approach. Many permutations have been attempted, including escalating hostilities to gain an advantage at the negotiating table, and maintaining military operations while talking.[29] Each shift in emphasis has been a response to past successes and failures. Clearly, it has been hard and costly to militarily degrade FARC, and to fight it into anything approaching a compromise.

Each prong of Colombia's approach has been honed over time. Security operations have improved by reducing the freedom accorded to right-wing paramilitaries and making Colombia's army operations more effective through US support. Negotiations have also varied between maximalist and more focused negotiation agendas.[30] These changes only matter, in a strategic sense, when lined up against one another. The threat or actuality of war has meant that every period of dialogue has unfolded against a backdrop of security measures. And even during military surges, the ultimate goal has been to impose a deal on FARC.

Turkey: belatedly opening a political track with the PKK

Over three decades Turkey has experienced a great many changes in its political life, economic standing and regional position – but its long war with the PKK has remained an open sore. It has been a brutal affair, with the total death toll of military personnel, civilians and PKK fighters estimated to be 30,000–40,000.[31] Turkey initially relied exclusively on security measures. Its military fought the PKK for control of the Kurdish-populated southeast, and attacked PKK strongholds in Iraq. After a bad start in the 1980s, by the 1990s the military had broken the PKK's hold over the southeast, pushing it into its northern Iraqi sanctuaries. PKK leader Abdullah Ocalan was captured in 1999, after the Syrian regime gave him up. Even if it had not been *destroyed*, the PKK had at least been displaced. Turkey's military presided over a victory of sorts, but at a huge cost in lives and displaced people.

Without a political dimension to its strategy, however, Turkey could not end the war. Its security-focused response could never address the political and socio-economic roots of the PKK's cause – Kurdish alienation from the state, and Kurdish feelings of deprivation relative to the rest of Turkey. Without some kind of negotiation process the PKK would never feel compelled to abandon violence. In the 1980s, and for much of the 1990s, the military's dominance of the state ensured that its preferred diagnosis of the PKK – as a security threat, deserving only to be met with force – endured. Politicians' attempts to talk to the PKK faced military censure and were short-lived.

It was not until the 2000s that Turkey tried to sustain a political track. Under the Justice and Development Party (AKP), a moderately Islamist political movement, and the prime minister, Recep Tayyip Erdogan (2003–14; president since 2014), Turkey eased its restrictions on its Kurdish population, in part to allow the AKP to chase their votes. An additional influence was Turkey's EU accession bid, which, although stalled, had for a time involved meeting EU accession criteria on such matters as minority rights. Turkey also negotiated with the PKK, talking to Ocalan and PKK leaders based in Iraq. This diversification in strategy mirrored the diminishing hold of the military over the state under the AKP, and the evolving nature of the state.

Despite rebalancing its strategy, Turkey has struggled to contend with the simultaneous undertakings of engaging in dialogue while intermittently fighting the PKK. Regional instability has further complicated matters. The PKK has adroitly exploited the transnational nature of the Kurdish cause, using sovereign borders and regional rivalries to help it survive. Wars in Iraq and Syria, and regional tensions involving Iran – countries with large Kurdish populations – have complicated the dynamic between Turkey and the PKK. Seemingly vacillating between bouts of making peace or war, the various strands of Turkey's approach to the PKK, always entwined, have only become knottier. Using a variety of approaches to support one another, and to move the conflict to an end, has been beyond Turkey. Examining how this intractability has arisen is instructive.

A brutal war: failing to coerce, let alone eliminate, the PKK (1984–1992)

Explaining just why the Turkish military became fixated on destroying the PKK goes hand in hand with explaining the roots of the PKK's insurrection. The two must be located in Turkish history. The Republic of Turkey came into being in 1923 under Mustafa Kemal Atatürk's military leadership, out of the ruins of the Ottoman Empire. The new Turkish state was founded on the premise of a populace bound by a secular, civic Turkish nationalism, with no official recognition of ethnic or religious sub-groups. Following the trauma of the First World War, after which Ottoman territory was carved up by the Triple Entente powers and Greece, the new Turkish state was fearful of further territorial fragmentation.

Understood in these terms, Kurdish nationalism in any form – violent or not – was an existential threat to Turkey's unity of people and territory. The Kurds, who had enjoyed a degree of autonomy under Ottoman rule, were now an unrecognised minority. This provoked Kurdish rebellions in the 1920s and 1930s, each of which was suppressed. In the decades that followed, the Turkish state tried to assimilate its Kurds, offering them the carrot of modernisation, but also using the stick of denying them linguistic, cultural and political freedoms.[32] There were no more Kurdish rebellions until Ocalan formed the PKK in 1978. A former student at Ankara University, Ocalan's Marxist–Leninist ideology conveyed how the PKK envisaged its struggle – as a liberation campaign against a colonising, occupying state presence. The urban, educated PKK would be the vanguard, fomenting an uprising among the largely agrarian Kurds of the southeast.[33] Control of this population would therefore be a precursor to strategic success for both sides.

The state was caught by surprise when the PKK began its war in 1984. President Kenan Evren (1980–89) wanted to comprehensively defeat the PKK: 'The snake must be killed while its head is small.'[34] This proved to be beyond the capabilities of the security forces. The gendarmerie, responsible for containing rural unrest, bore the initial brunt of fighting the PKK, but struggled to contain the PKK's blend of rural insurgency and urban subversion. So too did Turkey's conscript army, which was not nimble enough to pursue PKK fighters. Snow and mountainous terrain forced the war into a seasonal cycle, with Turkish forces only able to hunt the PKK during the warmer months.[35]

To marshal its defence of the southeast, insurgency-hit areas were placed under an emergency law ('OHAL', its Turkish acronym). The OHAL allowed security forces to drain the PKK of its support network by arbitrarily evicting Kurds from their villages. The extent of the displacement was huge, and in 2005 it was estimated that, of 5,000 settlements in existence before 1985, inhabitants from 3,848 had been wholly or partially displaced.[36] Those Kurds who stayed put were forced to join a state-sponsored civilian militia called the Village Guard, pitting them against the PKK. Village Guard recruitment drew on landowning tribes to whom the Marxist PKK posed a threat, offering recruits weapons, a salary and bonuses for any PKK members they killed. By the mid-1990s, 60,000 had been recruited. Some joined to settle scores or to be pardoned for crimes, but the PKK branded all Village Guards collaborators.[37]

According to Human Rights Watch, these measures amounted to a policy of 'draft or destroy'.[38] Given how hard it was to target the PKK, the state was in effect coercing the population among whom the PKK moved. This approach proved counterproductive. Security forces alienated a great many Kurds with forced displacement, which, in conjunction with PKK reprisals against Village Guards, exacerbated their fears and anxieties. The Kurds were caught between the two sides, each seemingly as brutal as the other. An outbreak of popular riots began in 1990 and spread across the southeast. The PKK stood to gain from this groundswell of Kurdish anger, reaching the apex of its powers in the early 1990s as its territorial hold across southeast Turkey expanded.

Talks: Ozal's abortive attempt to broaden the policy mix (1993)

For Ocalan, converting these gains into a positive outcome for the PKK required dialogue with the state. While the PKK began as a secessionist movement, it later altered its goal to greater Kurdish autonomy. This reflected Ocalan's pragmatism, with his ultimate goal being to force negotiations over the status of Turkey's Kurds. The onus for starting talks, however, was on the state: the PKK would have to wait for an offer to negotiate. This, in turn, would depend on the ascendency of a Turkish leader who could overcome the military's deeply held aversion to dialogue.

The first leader to explore the political track was Turgut Ozal, who served as prime minister (1983–89) and then president (1989–93). Ozal had burnished his credentials as an adroit manager of Turkey's security policy during the 1990–91 First Gulf War by joining the US-led coalition against Saddam Hussein's regime. As Ozal's international reputation grew, he felt sufficiently emboldened domestically to challenge the

General Staff over what to do about the PKK.[39] Ozal reduced Kurdish-language restrictions, explored investing in the south-east to assuage Kurdish poverty and, for the first time in official discourse, recognised the Kurds as a distinct minority. And Ozal opened a channel to Ocalan, using Iraqi Kurds as inter-mediaries. Ocalan responded to Ozal's overture by announcing a unilateral ceasefire in March 1993.

Then, one month later, Ozal died suddenly of a heart attack. Negotiations were stillborn and hostilities quickly resumed. After this brief flirtation with a political process, the military quickly reasserted control over strategy. Ozal's successor, Süleyman Demirel (1993–2000), let relations with the Iraqi Kurds slide. Demirel's prime minister, Tansu Ciller (1993–96), broached public discussion of allowing Kurdish-language broadcasting and a 'Basque model' of autonomy, but she was admonished by senior military figures, who asserted that only the military could discuss such matters.[40]

From the moment the insurgency began, Turkey's military had responded in a manner that reflected its institutional ethos. A fear of Turkey's territorial dismemberment by external or internal enemies was inculcated in its officers. By studying Atatürk's war of independence, the officers understood their duty as prevent-ing another Turkish decline. As custodians of a unified, secular Turkey, they lacked any concept of accommodating separatist ethno-religious elements in the state.[41] The Kemalist ideology, essential to the formation of the Turkish state, enshrined hostil-ity towards Kurdish nationalism. Even when the military was not in power (as it had been after coups in 1960, 1971 and 1980), it could still dominate civilian politicians, especially on national-security issues. Official discourse would focus on the terrorist aspects of the PKK, placing little focus on the PKK as a product of Kurdish grievances, and only mentioning a loosely defined 'southeast problem', not a 'Kurdish problem'.[42]

The military reasserts control and coerces the PKK (1994– 2004)

In the second half of the 1990s the military began to achieve results. Doctrinal reforms played a role in refining Turkish tactics for countering the guerrillas. The large-scale sweeps of territory relied on previously were supplemented by small teams of Turkish soldiers pursuing the PKK into its mountainous hideouts, and fighting on through the winter. In addition, special-forces teams were let loose in the southeast. The Ozel Tim, recruited from PKK defectors, right-wing zealots and JITEM, the gendarmerie intelligence, cast their net wide, detaining and killing PKK fighters, but also Kurdish nationalists and journalists alike.[43]

The PKK's attempts to emphasise its political credentials at this time fell on deaf ears. A 'Kurdistan Parliament in Exile' was formed in 1995, meeting in locations across Europe and urging a peaceful solution, but at the same time refusing to denounce the PKK's armed struggle.[44] Instead, Turkey's military was relying on a more expansive, more brutal response to erode the PKK's hold over the southeast.

In 1995 Turkish forces retook Diyarbakır, the centre of Kurdish nationalism in Turkey. According to Lieutenant-General Hasan Kundakçı, 'We had cleaned the inside; the next step was the outside.'[45] The army pressed home its advantage, attacking PKK sanctuaries in Iraq by staging a series of large-scale landholding incursions. In October 1992 Turkey deployed 15,000 troops to Iraq. This was followed by major incursions in 1995 and 1997, each of which did much to pressure the PKK. But Turkish forces were partly reliant on the support of the Kurds of northern Iraq to help isolate the PKK – and their support was not always forthcoming. Never quite able to corner and destroy the PKK, Turkey's military had to content itself with periodically striking PKK sanctuaries in Iraq's Qandil mountain range – something it has done with airpower ever since.[46]

Turkey's military scored a coercive success against Syria, where Ocalan was living. President Hafez al-Assad (1970–2000) had supported the PKK to offset Syria's perceived vulnerabilities against Turkey, which dwarfed Syria in size. In 1998 Turkey massed its troops at the Syrian border and threatened to invade, unless Ocalan was surrendered. Syria calculated that the price of supporting the PKK was too high and acquiesced to Turkish demands, signing an accord to cease supporting the PKK, and expelling Ocalan.[47] After a spell in Greece, Ocalan fled to Kenya (with Greek assistance) in February 1999, but was detained in Nairobi by Kenyan officials, and eventually given to Turkish officials.

What followed would divide opinion. Reflecting a hard line, Lieutenant-General Altay Tokat has said that 'the government made a historic mistake by not executing [Ocalan]. The mistake was to believe in his promises. That is what all the terrorists say after they are captured: they love the nation and promise to be helpful.'[48] Ocalan did in fact receive a death sentence, but his life was spared as Turkey revoked the death penalty to meet EU accession criteria. Imprisoned on Imralı Island, in the Marmara Sea, with access only to his lawyers, Ocalan would remain the PKK's figurehead. Daily command fell to Murat Karayılan and Cemil Bayık in Iraq's Qandil mountains. But Ocalan's edicts, issued from jail via his lawyers, still carried weight among those Kurds for whom he remained a living folk hero.

Incarcerated, Ocalan proved to be a pragmatist. He renounced Marxism, asked the PKK to suspend violence and advocated a state in which Kurds lived as equals with Turks. Between 1999 and 2004 PKK violence remained low. But in June 2004, Ocalan called an end to the PKK ceasefire after declaring his frustration at the lack of political advancement. Long desiring the ear of the state, Ocalan now had regular contact with officials. But no substantive talks had occurred. The dominant voices in Ankara lacked the will, and an opportunity to deal with the PKK while it was on the back foot was squandered.[49]

The AKP: starting a political track, but still fighting the PKK (2005–2014)

Erdogan's election win in 2002 began a transformative era in Turkish politics. The AKP's popular mandate was solidified after it was re-elected in 2007 and 2011. Erdogan was sufficiently emboldened to challenge the military and its Kemalist paradigms, using the EU's criteria for accession as a rationale for reforming Turkey's civil–military relations and its minority rights. Turkish strategy gradually diversified, albeit motivated by a desire to win Kurdish votes for the AKP and to undercut the General Staff, as well as to undercut the PKK with a promise of peace. Initially, the signs were good.

Branded by the AKP as a 'democratic opening', restrictions were eased on Kurdish rights of linguistic and cultural expression in the media and in schools.[50] The AKP government faced criticisms from Kemalist political parties and the military that these concessions were rewarding PKK violence. An even thornier issue, politically and practically speaking, would be whether to talk to the PKK. Opinions varied. Voices favouring a peace process argued that 'the PKK will have to be part of any solution' because, 'as well as being a well-organised group it also carries with it considerable support at the grass-roots levels'.[51] Conversely, voices closer to the military argued that 'the conflict-resolution process is hampered because the [PKK] does not wish to or cannot move away from what it was'. Consequently, the way to stop the PKK from spoiling a conflict-resolution process would be 'the removal of the PKK's safe haven in northern Iraq'.[52]

In the end Turkey did a bit of both. In October 2007, after suffering its largest military death toll in a decade that month at the hands of the PKK, when 27 soldiers were killed, Turkey responded with an aerial bombardment against PKK positions, followed in February 2008 by a land incursion into northern Iraq. But Turkey was also exploring a multilevel dialogue process. Its officials continued to speak to Ocalan in Imralı, while international mediators were in contact with the PKK in Iraq. And a secret channel was opened for Turkish intelligence officials to meet PKK representatives in Oslo in 2009–10. In a leaked recording of a mediated dialogue session in Oslo, National Intelligence Organization (MIT) undersecretary Hakan Fidan was introduced as 'special representative' to Erdogan, who Fidan said was sincere about resolving the Kurdish question. Fidan asked the PKK to begin a ceasefire, but in response, the PKK representatives asked for a cessation of military operations.[53] The leaked recording caused a scandal in Turkey, scuppering the talks and leaving the AKP open to criticism from pro-Kemalist parties that it was appeasing the PKK.

The level of turmoil in the region has greatly complicated the context in which the PKK is dealt with. In Iraq, after Saddam Hussein's fall in 2003, the Kurdish Regional Government (KRG) of northern Iraq became politically and economically ascendant. Turkey responded by developing strong economic ties with the KRG, but could not persuade the KRG to pursue the PKK. The Iraqi Kurdish political parties making up the KRG were keenly aware of the fragility of their own arrangements, having experienced an intra-Kurdish civil war in the 1990s involving their two main factions. But it was the outbreak of war in Syria in 2011, and the rise of Islamic State, also known as ISIS or ISIL, in 2014, that would alter the regional picture beyond recognition.

As the wars in Iraq and Syria have merged into an interconnected conflict, the Kurds of the region have become a focal point. In Iraq, the conflict has embroiled the KRG's security forces, the *pershmerga*, who have fought ISIS. And it has drawn in Syria's Kurdish armed group, the Democratic Union Party (PYD), which has links to the PKK. The urgency of the battle against ISIS, and US backing for the *pershmerga* in this fight, has alarmed Turkey. It has exacerbated Turkish fears that this mixture of Kurdish groups senses the potential for a Kurdish state to emerge from the fragmentation of Iraq and Syria.

The complex regional picture means that much more is required than Ankara simply aligning its threats and incentives towards the PKK in order to reach a deal. Many factors would have to coincide favourably. A hypothetical deal with the PKK would be likely to involve its abandoning violence in exchange for Turkey instigating constitutional changes to address the issue of Kurdish rights, and perhaps granting a measure of Kurdish autonomy in the southeast.[54] Even if Erdogan has at times genuinely sought a deal with the PKK, when the security situation has worsened, the military has argued that any measures that reward PKK violence risk fragmenting Turkey. Even Erdogan could not completely ignore these concerns and has latterly come to back a more militarised response. This has left Turkey with a mix of policies: of an enduring security response balanced with intermittent political and economic outreach.

It is hard for the Turkish state to accept that the PKK's armed struggle has, over decades, carved out a political space for discussion of the Kurdish issue in Turkey. Turkey finds it instinctively hard to countenance allowing the PKK to occupy this political space. Compounding this impasse, the PKK's dominance of the Kurdish cause has prevented the rise of non-violent Kurdish groups. Ankara has had few credible Kurdish moderates, free of PKK influence, with whom to bargain over the position of Turkey's Kurds. Judicial authorities have dele-gitimised successive Kurdish political parties, accusing them of having links to terrorism – a charge they have struggled to avoid given the long shadow the PKK has cast over the Kurdish cause.[55] Turkey would be greatly strengthened, domestically and internationally, by ending its confrontation with the PKK. But, as the conflict enters its fourth decade, Turkey's strategic approach, for all its evolutions, seems short of definitive outcomes.

Chasing political settlements with armed groups

Military campaigns can degrade armed groups but may be unable to defeat them. Even from a point of stalemate, states can struggle to pressure an armed group into making a deal. Such an outcome is certainly not impossible, but as the conflicts in Colombia and Turkey illustrate, a great many factors have to fall into place for there to be any progress. Not least, the state needs to summon and sustain enough political will to push for a deal. In doing so, it has to accept the blood debt it has accrued over the course of a long war, and stomach the concessions that it may need to make to a hated enemy. The armed group must also be able to muster sufficient support to present a unified front that is prepared to negotiate. And if neighbouring states have played either witting or unwitting roles in abetting the insurgency, then the number of supporting pieces that have to fall into place only multiplies.

Given these complexities, it may seem churlish to point to a state's failure to manage its own policy mix. And yet, without some mastery of the various instruments they are bringing to bear on the problem, states may simply miss their opportunity to end a conflict, as rarely as such opportunities might arise. States must possess clarity about what they want, and under-stand the trade-offs between different components of their approach. In this way, they can employ their security, political, economic and other responses in a mutually supportive way, increasing the prospects for advancing their aims, even if this does not guarantee them a decisive success.

Whether states choose to 'talk and then fight', or 'fight and then talk', the outcome may be the same – states may end up oscillating between dialogue and war, sometimes pursuing both at the same time, but with little to clearly show for their efforts in either case. In long confrontations with armed groups, breaking out of this cycle can be a challenge. And failure to do so can leave states forever managing the problem, rather than definitively addressing it, as the armed group becomes a fixture on the domestic and perhaps the regional landscapes.

Notes

1   William Zartman, *Elusive Peace: Negotiating an End to Civil Wars* (Washington DC: Brookings Institution, 1995), p. 8.

2   Mao Zedong, *On Guerrilla Warfare* (Washington DC: USMC, 1989), p. 22.

3   Estimates of the size of FARC are not always consistent. See International Crisis Group, 'Ending Colombia's FARC Conflict: Dealing the Right Card' (26 March 2009), p. 7.

4   For an account of the roots of Colombian political violence, see Nazih Richani, *Systems of Violence: The Political Economy of War and Peace in Colombia* (Albany, NY: State University of New York Press, Second Edition, 2013), pp. 11–34.

5   *Ibid.*, p. 7.

6   Francisco Leal Buitrago, 'Armed Actors in the Colombian Conflict', in Kees Koonings and Dirk Kruijt (eds), *Armed Actors: Organised* *Violence and State Failure in Latin America* (London: Zed Books, 2004), pp. 87–105.

7   James J. Brittain, *Revolutionary Social Change in Colombia: The Origin and Direction of the FARC-EP* (New York: Pluto Press, 2010), pp. 1–30.

8   International Crisis Group, 'Colombia's Elusive Quest for Peace' (26 March 2002), pp. 5–6; Carlo Nasi, 'Colombia's Peace Process 1982–2002', p. 50 and Mark Chernik, 'The FARC at the Negotiating Table', both in Virginia M. Bouvier (ed.), *Colombia: Building Peace in a Time of War* (Washington DC: United States Institute for Peace, 2009), pp. 50, 88–9.

9   Buitrago, 'Armed Actors in the Colombian Conflict', in Koonings and Kruijt, *Armed Actors: Organised Violence and State Failure in Latin America*, pp. 87–105; Richani, *Systems of Violence: The Political*

Economy of War and Peace in Colombia, pp. 35–8.

10 Nasi, 'Colombia's Peace Process 1982–2002', pp. 39, 64.

11 *Ibid.*, p. 49; International Crisis Group, 'Colombia's Elusive Quest for Peace', p. 6.

12 Nasi, 'Colombia's Peace Process 1982–2002', p. 40.

13 International Crisis Group, 'Colombia's New Armed Groups' (10 May 2007).

14 International Crisis Group, 'Colombia's Elusive Quest for Peace', pp. 20–6; IISS, *The FARC Files: Venezuela, Ecuador and the Secret Archive of 'Raúl Reyes'* (London: IISS, 2011), p. 213.

15 Chernik, 'The FARC at the Negotiating Table', pp. 73, 82–3. See also pp. 9–10.

16 *Ibid.*, p. 68.

17 International Crisis Group, 'Ending Colombia's FARC Conflict: Dealing the Right Card', pp. 7–11.

18 'Colombia: New Approach to Guerrilla Threat', IISS *Strategic Comments*, vol. 19, no. 30, October 2013.

19 Chernik, 'The FARC at the Negotiating Table', p. 92.

20 Nasi, 'Colombia's Peace Process 1982–2002', pp. 54–60.

21 Jeffery H. Michaels, *The Discourse Trap and the US Military* (Basingstoke: Palgrave Macmillan, 2013), pp. 70–1.

22 Dana Priest, 'Covert Action in Colombia: US Intelligence, GPS Bomb Kits Help Latin American Nation Cripple Rebel Forces', *Washington Post*, 21 December 2013, http://www.washingtonpost.com/sf/investigative/2013/12/21/covert-action-in-colombia/?hpid=z1.

23 Priest, 'Covert Action in Colombia'.

24 'Colombia and the FARC: Digging In for Peace', *The Economist*, 1 June 2013; 'Colombia: New Approach to Guerrilla Threat', IISS *Strategic Comments*.

25 National Centre for Historical Memory, http://www.centrodememoriahistorica.gov.co/micrositios/informeGeneral/estadisticas.html.

26 'Colombia and the FARC: Digging In for Peace', pp. 51–2.

27 'Colombia's Armed Forces: General Exit', *The Economist*, 22 February 2014, p. 45.

28 IISS *Strategic Comments*, 'Colombia: New Approach to Guerrilla Threat'.

29 Chernik, 'The FARC at the Negotiating Table', p. 92.

30 Nasi, 'Colombia's Peace Process 1982–2002', p. 63.

31 Turkish Ministry of Foreign Affairs, http://www.mfa.gov.tr/pkk_kongra-gel.en.mfa, estimates 30,000 Turkish citizens have perished, whereas a figure of 35,000–40,000 dead is estimated by Vera Eccarius-Kelly, *The Militant Kurds: A Dual Strategy for Freedom* (Santa Barbara, CA: Praeger, 2010), p. 19.

32 David McDowell, *The Kurds: A Nation Divided* (London: Minority Rights Publications, 1992); James Ciment, *The Kurds: State and Minority in Turkey, Iraq and Iran* (New York: Facts On File, Inc., 1996); Henri J. Barkey and Graham E. Fuller, *Turkey's Kurdish Question* (Lanham, MD/Boulder, CO/New York/Oxford: Rowman and Littlefield Publishers, 1998); Metin Heper, *The State and Kurds in Turkey: The Question of Assimilation* (London: Palgrave Macmillan, 2007).

33 Ismet G. Imset, *The PKK: A Report on Separatist Violence in Turkey 1973–1992* (Ankara: Turkish Daily News Publications, 1992); Aliza Marcus, *Blood and Belief: the PKK and the Kurdish Fight for Independence* (New York: New York University Press, 2007).

34 Evren (1984) quoted in Marcus, *Blood and Belief*, p. 82.

35 Umit Ozdag, *The PKK and Low Intensity Conflict in Turkey*, Ankara Paper 5 (London: Frank Cass, 2003).

36 Kerim Yildiz, *The Kurds in Turkey: EU Accession and Human Rights* (London: Pluto Press, 2005), p. 77.

37 Hugh Pope and Nicole Pope, *Turkey Unveiled: Atatürk and After* (London: John Murray, 1997), p. 269; Marcus, *Blood and Belief*, p. 98; Ozdag, *The PKK and Low Intensity Conflict in Turkey*, p. 22.

38 'Turkey: Forced Displacement of Ethnic Kurds from Southeastern Turkey', Human Rights Watch, vol. 6, no. 12, October 1994; Joost Jongerden, *The Settlement Issue in Turkey and the Kurds* (Leiden/Boston: Brill Academic Publishers, 2007), p. 96.

39 Steven Cook, *Ruling But Not Governing: The Military and Political Development in Egypt, Algeria, and Turkey* (Baltimore: Johns Hopkins Press, 2007), pp. 114–15.

40 Barkey and Fuller, *Turkey's Kurdish Question*, pp. 136–7.

41 Mehmet Ali Birand, *Shirts of Steel: An Anatomy of the Turkish Armed Forces* (London/New York: I.B. Tauris, 1991), pp. 57–85.

42 Murat Somer, 'Why Aren't Kurds Like Scots and Turks Like Brits? Moderation and Democracy in the Kurdish Question', *Cooperation and Conflict*, vol. 43, no. 2, June 2008, pp. 220–49.

43 Ozdag, *The PKK and Low Intensity Conflict in Turkey*; Barkey and Fuller, *Turkey's Kurdish Question*, p. 148.

44 Paul White, *Primitive Rebels or Revolutionary Modernizers? The Kurdish National Movement in Turkey* (London/New York: Zed Books, 2000), pp. 177–8; Barkey and Fuller, *Turkey's Kurdish Question*, p. 27.

45 Kundakçi translated from Fikret Bila, *The Commanders' Front* (Istanbul: Dogan Publishing, 2010), pp. 105–10.

46 Ozdag, *The PKK and Low Intensity Conflict in Turkey*; Ersel Aydinli and Nihat Ali Ozcan, 'The Conflict Resolution and Counterterrorism Dilemma: Turkey Faces its Kurdish Question', *Terrorism and Political Violence*, vol. 23, no. 3, 2011, pp. 438–50.

47 Mahmut Bali Aykan, 'Turkish–Syrian Crisis of October 1998: A Turkish View', *Middle East Policy*, vol. 6, no. 4, June 1999.

48 Interview with Lt.-Gen. Altay Tokat, translated from Bila, *The Commanders' Front*, pp. 124–5.

49 Michael Gunter, *The Kurds Ascending* (New York: Palgrave Macmillan, 2008), pp. 72–84.

50 Robert Olson, *Blood, Beliefs and Ballots: the Management of Kurdish Nationalism in Turkey 2007–2009* (Costa Mesa, CA: Mazda Publishers, 2009); Murat Somer and Evangelos G. Liaras, 'Turkey's New Kurdish Opening: Religious versus Secular Values', *Middle East Policy*, vol. 17, no. 2, Summer 2010.

51 Interview with Kerim Yildiz, Director, Kurdish Human Rights Project, London, 24 May 2011.

52 Aydinli and Ozcan, 'The Conflict Resolution and Counterterrorism Dilemma: Turkey Faces its Kurdish Question', pp. 446, 450.

53 'Alleged PKK Talks Tape Rattles Turkish Politics', *Hurriyet Daily News*, 14 September 2011. The 47-minute recording of the meeting is online: http://hevallo.blogspot.com/2011/09/leaked-oslo-5-video-peace-leak.html.

54 F. Stephen Larrabee, 'Turkey's New Kurdish Opening', *Survival: Global Politics and Strategy*, vol. 55, no. 5, October–November 2013, pp. 133–46.

55 Nicole F. Watts, *Activists in Office: Kurdish Politics and Protest in Turkey* (Washington DC: University of Washington Press, 2011).

CHAPTER THREE

The ruthless pragmatism of being selective and deceptive

The West rejects militant struggles for freedom too readily. The US and Europe too often equate all militancy with terrorism.

Pervez Musharraf, 2006[1]

No-one has a moral right to tell us to talk to child killers. Why don't you meet Osama Bin Laden, invite him to Brussels or to the White House and engage in talks, ask him what he wants and give it to him so he leaves you in peace?

Vladimir Putin, 2004[2]

Judging which armed groups are truly abhorrent, and which could be tolerated under certain circumstances, is a matter of perspective. It is also a matter of policy choice. States may be willing to go to extraordinary lengths to be selective, and possibly deceptive, in order to work with some armed groups while fighting others. Facing a seemingly intractable conflict, these states may be willing to pay a high price to safeguard their long-term strategic interests. They may be resistant to voices from abroad contending that such a path is devoid of moral scruple. And these states may be quite content to deal with the Devil, so to speak, by talking to some armed groups to try to isolate those militants who appear to them even more devilish.

There is a ruthless logic of pragmatism at work in the conflicts examined here. In Pakistan's confrontation with Islamist armed groups after 9/11, and Russia's confrontations in the North Caucusus, these states have made judgements about which armed groups to work with and which to fight. It is an approach that, by definition, demands a blend of fighting and talking, and brings to the fore the importance of deception, since the state's real objectives may simply be to buy time, or to displace the threat. A negotiated and equitable political settlement is certainly not the objective that is sought here.

Selectivity has been the key theme in Pakistan's strategic approach: in the face of multiple and factionalised armed groups, it has sought to treat each group differently. In a very a different context, in Chechnya, Russia anointed former rebels to encourage them to fight more extreme elements. These are risky, perhaps even cynical approaches – by accommodating some militants, while leaving others to run amok, problems can be stored up for the future. The persistence of insecurity in Pakistan and the North Caucasus attests to this. The focus here is on the extraordinary measures states may take to be selective, and at times deceptive, in working with some armed groups while fighting others, and how these states have used multiple policy tracks to advance these aims.

Russia: playing politics and waging war to quell Chechnya's rebellion

The tactics that the Russian state has used to quell challenges to its authority appear brutal, and perhaps even mindlessly so, to Western sensibilities. This has been true in the Chechen separatist wars that began in 1994. After a decade, around 160,000 civilians and combatants from all sides had been killed.[3] At first glance, this horrific toll implies that Russia relied purely on military means to forcibly retain the breakaway republic. Moscow's crackdown in the First Chechen War (1994–96), and in the Second Chechen War that began in 1999, goes some way to creating the impression that Russia was utterly uncompromising.

On closer examination, Russia's strategy has in fact involved controlled compromise. Russia's broader strategic response in Chechnya has comprised two streams: a brutal security response paired with a political strategy of co-opting those Chechen rebels Moscow deemed to be more palatable to deal with. After Russia's army reoccupied the Chechen capital Grozny in 2000, Moscow installed a new local leader, Akhmad Kadyrov, a rebel turned Russian loyalist, who was later replaced by his son, Ramzan Kadyrov. Local power was delegated to the Kadyrov clan, as was the task of fighting the rebels responsible for terror attacks such as the September 2004 Beslan school siege, which gave rise to President Vladimir Putin's (2000–08; 2012–) rejection of talks with 'child killers'. Thus, Russia's policy mix involved a prolonged interplay between its security measures and manipulation of the politics of Chechnya's rebellion. All the while, Putin would attempt to cultivate an uncompromising image in the face of terrorists and secessionists.

If viewed through the narrow prism of the Kremlin's initial aims, these policies have worked. Russia retained its sovereignty over Chechnya, preventing further fragmentation of its territory after 1991. It imposed something of a victor's peace on Chechnya's rulers,[4] but bought this outcome at a price. Firstly, it left Moscow reliant on its vassal, Akhmad Kadyrov, to ensure that Chechnya's post-war reconstruction could be presented as a success story. Secondly, the brutal nature of Russia's security crackdown contributed to a spreading of militancy out of Chechnya and across neighbouring regions. The wider North Caucasus region suffered an ongoing insurgency, while Russia's heartlands experienced occasional terrorist attacks. The roots of this North Caucasus rebellion lie in the initial spark of the Chechen rebellion but, over time, it has become far more Islamist in tone. It is an ambiguous outcome, perhaps, but one that Russia has advanced towards through a policy mix of war and politics.

The military response: First and Second Chechen Wars (1994–2000)

Chechen resistance to Russian domination has a strong historical pedigree. So too do pragmatic Russian responses to co-opting these rebels. Leo Tolstoy's nineteenth-century novel *Hadji Murat* tells the story of Chechen rebel Murat who decides to switch sides, joining the Russians to save his family.[5] In Tolstoy's era, Tsarist Russia fought to annex the Caucasus. Russian general Alexei Yermolov founded Grozny as his headquarters in 1818. The Chechens fought back under Imam Shamil, who aimed to evict the Russians and establish an Islamic state. In 1859, Shamil was captured, his rebellion subdued and Chechnya later annexed. It was not until 1922, several years after the collapse of Tsarist Russia, that a Chechen autonomous region was established. It did not survive the Soviet era. In 1944 Stalin deported much of the Chechen population to Siberia and Central Asia, having accused them of collaborating with Nazi Germany.[6]

The mountainous North Caucasus region, which extends from the Black Sea to the Caspian Sea, has long been a frontier of Russian power. The region contains a patchwork of communities with strong local identities, of which the Chechens are one such group. The geostrategic importance of the lands they inhabit has, if anything, grown since the Russian Federation replaced the USSR. While the USSR's southern border was with Turkey and Iran, today the Russian Federation's southern border is between its North Caucasus region and the post-Soviet states of Georgia, Armenia and Azerbaijan. Thus, when Chechen separatists declared independence to break away from Moscow's rule amid the collapse of the USSR, a deeply rooted history of conflict was aggravated. Both sides were willing to fight hard: Moscow for the new boundaries of its territorial integrity, and the Chechen rebels for their first genuine opportunity for independence in decades.

Mutinous Red Army officers General Dzhokhar Dudayev and Colonel Aslan Maskhadov, both ethnic Chechens, led the rebels. With Moscow in disarray in 1991, Chechnya was proclaimed to be independent of Russia, with Dudayev as president and Maskhadov his chief of staff. For three years Chechnya was run as a de facto independent state, albeit floundering in the economic turmoil of the end of communism. Dudayev struggled to establish a state apparatus, but his biggest failure was in negotiating with Moscow over Chechnya's future status. Rather than make concessions, he threatened war if separatist aspirations were not granted.[7] By 1994, Dudayev already faced a local Moscow-backed armed Chechen opposition. That year, Kremlin hawks prevailed on president Boris Yeltsin (1991–99) to crush the separatists with Russia's army.[8]

The First Chechen War lasted from December 1994 to August 1996. Yeltsin had hoped for a brief military campaign to reassert the territorial integrity of the Russian Federation, and to boost his own popularity. Instead, the war was a catastrophe for Russia's army, which suffered a bloody defeat. Well-dug-in rebels destroyed Russia's conscript-manned armoured columns as they advanced along Grozny's streets, many of which had been reduced to rubble by a prior bombardment. There was a rot at the heart of Russia's military in the post-Soviet era, as its poor tactics and rout in the face of Chechen rebels showed.[9]

Terror reprisal attacks were already a feature of the conflict. Chechen rebels took the fight to Russia, outside the war zone. In June 1995, militant Islamist leader Shamil Basayev led an attack on Buddenovsk hospital, around 110 kilometres north of Chechnya. As Russia's army responded, Basayev escaped, but at least 120 others would die, the majority of whom were civilians. The Buddenovsk siege, and the bloody military deadlock in Grozny, left the Russian state reeling. It opened the path to the August 1996 Khasavyurt Accords. For the first time since the conflict began, Yeltsin agreed to negotiate with the rebels. Sidestepping the matter of Chechnya's ultimate political status, Russian forces effectively ceded autonomy to the rebels, signed the accord and withdrew.[10]

Chechnya had become a symbol of the impotence of a former superpower. If the Russian Federation could not project power within its new borders, how could it possibly be expected to do so outside? Putin vowed to turn this situation around. Yeltsin, whose health was failing, had announced his resignation on New Year's Eve 1999. Putin, at that time prime minister (1999–2000), would preside over a response to the Chechen crisis that would invigorate his future presidency by appearing to decisively defeat the separatists. However, the Chechen rebels against whom he would wage war in the 2000s were of a more extremist Islamist bent than their forebears.

The initial wave of Chechen rebels had been nationalists. Dudayev and Maskhadov had sought a secular, nationalist Chechnya (albeit partly based on a line of demarcation between Muslim Chechnya and Orthodox Christian Russia). But their time as stewards of Chechnya's rebellion was passing. Russian forces had killed Dudayev in April 1996. This left Maskhadov to negotiate the Khasavyurt Accords. However, Maskhadov's authority faltered as he struggled to run a war-ravaged Chechnya, and as the Chechen cause became increasingly radical, inspired by extremists such as Basayev who wanted to take the fight to the Russians.[11] Jihadists from far and wide joined the cause, travelling to Chechnya as they had to Afghanistan in the 1980s, supplanting the nationalist core of the Chechen movement with a jihadist ideology.[12]

In August 1999, the month in which Putin became prime minister, Basayev led a major incursion into Dagestan, adjacent to Chechnya. Basayev wished to expand the conflict, seeking common cause with separatists in Dagestan who were also waging jihad against Russian authorities. As Russian forces counter-attacked, they refused Maskhadov's offer of help, because they believed he could not control Basayev.

The following month the war came to Russia's capital: 293 people were killed in a series of bomb attacks on apartment blocks in Moscow and other Russian cities. The authorities attributed these bombings to Chechen separatists, and used the resulting popular outrage to sustain public support to re-invade Chechnya. This narrative would later be challenged by former Federal Security Service (FSB) officer Alexander Litvinenko, who had defected to the UK, and by investigative journalist Anna Politkovskaya, both of whom alleged that the Russian state had been complicit in the bombings and used them as a *casus belli*.[13] Although it is impossible to evaluate the veracity of their claims, both were killed in 2006, Litvinenko by radiation poisoning in London and Politkovskaya in Moscow.

Russian troops re-entered Chechnya soon after the apartment bombings and fought to regain control of Grozny in 2000. Chechen rebels fled in large numbers to the surrounding hills. By the end of the year much of Chechnya was back in Russian possession.[14] Although this had seemingly been achieved by brute force, Russia's policy mix was about to diversify.

'Chechenisation': combining the political and security tracks (2001–2014)

There would be no peace process. Putin steadfastly refused to engage the separatists in negotiations over Chechnya's future. When Russian forces killed Maskhadov in March 2005, any remaining prospects for talks ended. Rather, Moscow's political strategy would involve circumventing those separatists it deemed irreconcilable, and choosing others it felt it could work with. By turning some rebels against the others, Moscow would in effect pick local proxies to run Chechnya on its behalf.

It did so by exploiting the sectarian fissures between Chechen Sufis, who practised a spiritual form of Islam and whose presence was rooted in the history of the North Caucasus, and extremist Salafi jihadists. The Chechen Sufi clergy found their power base challenged by the arrival of the Salafis, some of whom had come from the Middle East.[15] Russia played on this. Key Sufi leaders sided with Russia to stave off the Salafis. Mufti Akhmad Kadyrov was one such figure. In 1995 he had declared war on Russia, but later switched sides to support Russia's intervention and to resist the likes of Basayev. In March 2003 a referendum was held in Chechnya, the result of which was a vote in favour of remaining in the Russian Federation. Akhmad Kadyrov was named president of Chechnya in October 2003, but was assassinated in May 2004 in Grozny. His son Ramzan also sided with the Russian state and in 2007 Putin installed him as head of the Chechen Republic.

There was a nominal devolution of responsibilities from federal level to local. Chechnya had its own parliament and secured substantial federal money to rebuild Grozny after its devastation in the Chechen wars. The reality, however, was that Ramzan Kadyrov was Moscow's vassal. Having received political and economic rewards from Moscow, Kadyrov continued to fight Islamist separatists on Moscow's behalf. His armed groups, the *kadyrovtsy*, were former separatists and were later legitimised by Russian federal forces. The *kadyrovtsy* coerced other former insurgents to change sides, providing guarantees that they too could join the official security forces to fight the Salafis.[16] In this way, Russian soldiers extricated themselves and reoriented the conflict to an intra-Chechen affair. As author Sebastian Smith has observed, banditry in Chechnya 'expanded, diversified and nationalised'.[17]

The 'Chechenisation' strategy has carried risks for Moscow. 'The Kadyrov–Putin relationship is an extreme form of personal fealty', according to authors Hill and Gaddy.[18] The risk is that the tail comes to wag the dog. Some *siloviki* – Russian security personnel, such as those in the FSB – fear that Chechenisation has simply handed victory to the separatists:

> Putin struck a Faustian deal in Chechnya. It relies on Kadyrov remaining both invincible and loyal … by pursuing accommodation with the Kremlin, Kadyrov has managed to win more power from and over Moscow than the Chechen secessionists of the 1990s ever did by fighting for it.[19]

Indeed, Russian intelligence preferred to balance Kadyrov's influence with that of other pro-Russia Chechen units, such as Sulim Yamadayev's Vostok battalion and the Zapad battalion. But Kadyrov ruthlessly marginalised his rivals, fighting them until they no longer challenged him. Amid this murky intra-Chechen struggle, Yamadayev was assassinated in 2009 in Dubai, United Arab Emirates, to where he had moved having left Russia, and no killer was apprehended. In this way, Kadyrov ensured that he remained the essential local enabler of Moscow's policies.

Russia continued to suffer periodic terrorist attacks, which were ostensibly made worse by security forces' heavy-handed response. In the October 2002 Nord-Ost siege, 170 people were killed when Russian soldiers stormed a Moscow theatre that Chechen rebels had seized. Gas used by the soldiers to incapacitate the attackers may also have killed many hostages. In the September 2004 Beslan siege, Islamist separatists captured a school in North Ossetia. Again, the Russian security response was partly responsible for many of the 331 deaths that resulted from the operation to retake the school.

It was a talismanic moment, therefore, when Russian forces killed Basayev in July 2006, near the Ingushetia–North Ossetia border. Three years later Russia declared an official end to its 'counter-terrorism' operation in Chechnya. Symbolic though Basayev's killing had been, the terrorist attacks continued. In March 2010, suicide bombings on the Moscow underground killed 40 people. In January 2011 a suicide bomb at Moscow's Domodedovo airport killed 36. And, weeks before the start of the 2014 Sochi Winter Olympics, in December 2013, a series of suicide bombs struck the city of Volgograd.

The militant threat in the region had evolved. In 2007 an Islamist militant named Doku Umarov established a group called the Caucasus Emirate, which aimed to replace Russian rule in the North Caucasus with an Islamic state. The methods Russia had used to hold on to Chechnya had, in effect, displaced the problem, as violence flared up in the neighbouring regions of Dagestan and Ingushetia.

The Western world was reminded about this forgotten war when two brothers, Dzhokhar and Tamerlan Tsarnaev, who had come to the US from Dagestan and whose early lives had been scarred by the war there, bombed the Boston Marathon in April 2013.[20] Their early biographies were a reminder of the fact that the Russian state had been fighting a war in the North Caucasus, largely out of global view, for over a generation.

In a region where the scars of war are clear, the Russian state has apparently lacked a strategy for integrating its North Caucasus Muslims. As Dagestan and Ingushetia have absorbed large numbers of Chechens displaced by war, insurgency has also reached a wider area that includes North Ossetia, Kabardino-Balkaria, Karachay-Cherkessia and Stavropol Krai. Russia's response has remained fixed on killing insurgent leaders, with little focus on dealing with their motivations.[21] Putin's strategy has not sought to engage local people to assuage the matter of Muslim alienation in the North Caucasus.[22]

However, the brutality of the Chechen war is not the sole cause of Russia's violent Islamist challenge. There are deeper socio-economic issues, too. According to the 2010 census, Muslims constitute 10.9% of Russia's population; they tend to live in poorer, rural areas, and the Muslim birth rate is higher than that among other elements of the Russian population.[23] The Russian state duly faces a complex problem that blends religious, ethnic and secessionist grievances amid a potentially restive populace. Russia's stabilisation of Chechnya may have prevented this ethnically fragmented region from breaking away from Moscow's rule, but it has papered over the cracks of a potentially bigger series of problems.[24]

Russia's example shows that a political track can take many forms. It does not necessarily have to mean the pursuit of a just or equitable solution via a peace process. Russia has brutally pursued military victory, giving one faction of the Chechen uprising what it wanted – de facto autonomy, money, legitimacy – in return for helping to crush the less palatable rebels. The interconnectedness between the security response and the political challenge of governing Chechnya is instructive in relation to Russia's strategic predilection for confronting dissent.

Whether aspects of the Chechen 'solution' can be applied to other regions where Russia wishes to establish sovereign control is a pertinent question. Beyond Russia's borders – for example, in South Ossetia and Abkhazia (for control over which Russia challenged Georgia in 2008), and in Crimea and the Donbas (for control over which Russia challenged Ukraine in 2014) – Moscow has sought local militias to endorse its own policies. These are inter-state confrontations, with Russia wresting control of these territories from the Georgian and Ukrainian states. But it does not stretch the imagination to consider how Russian veterans of the Chechen war may have adapted an approach honed in the North Caucasus outside Russia's borders, too.

Pakistan: fighting and talking to Islamist militants since 9/11

The Pakistani state has managed to advance its strategic interests, as difficult as this may be for Western states to accept, having seen Pakistan duck its commitment to fight armed groups and perhaps even knowingly host Osama bin Laden. For the generals at Rawalpindi headquarters, however, exploiting the ambiguities inherent in talking while fighting became a strategy to buy them time and influence. Pakistan has played host to many Islamist armed groups. Some were state proxies that fought in Afghanistan, in order to buy Pakistan regional influence at the expense of its weaker neighbour, and in Kashmir, where Pakistan has wanted to challenge its perennial rival and antagonist, India. After the 9/11 attacks, the US told Pakistan to end its support for these proxy groups. For Pakistan's security agencies, however, this was not a straightforward choice. By taking on armed groups such as the Taliban and Lashkar-e-Taiba (LeT), Pakistan would risk losing an influential lever of its security apparatus. And it risked provoking a backlash of Islamist violence, all on behalf of US security objectives that Pakistan did not necessarily share.

Pakistan's response was at least partly duplicitous. While fighting some Islamist militants to appease the US, it retained channels of communication to others. Pakistan's armed forces would most energetically fight those armed groups it deemed as posing a direct threat to its national interest. Against others, it would be passive, slower in its military response, or would actively preserve their proxy potential. In some instances, Pakistan would fight armed groups that it would later appease.[25] In this way, Pakistan was attempting to triage the multiple threats it faced, including the threat of turning the US into an outright antagonist.

This was not a strategy born solely from perfidy. After 9/11 it may have seemed Pakistan's least bad option. General Pervez Musharraf, who served as president (2001–08) and also army chief of staff (1998–2007), mastered this strategy of talking and fighting. Understanding Pakistan's armed-group milieu to consist of numerous, separable factions, Musharraf attempted to sequentially bargain with and coerce different groups in turn. This was as much a self-preservation strategy as it was a Machiavellian gambit. Musharraf sought to limit Pakistan's involvement in what he saw as America's fight by keeping the peace with some groups while fighting others. As this case study shows, Musharraf's successors maintained his essential strategy.

However, there is a strong argument to be made that this strategy backfired. Between 2001 and 2014, more than 50,000 Pakistani civilians and combatants are estimated to have died in armed-group violence and in military counter-offensives.[26] Pakistan could not prevent the fighting from escalating and spreading, nor could it prevent a relentless suicide-bombing campaign. Pakistan would have to parry and retaliate against these blows, whether or not one characterises the state as being duplicitous in its dealings with the Islamist militants. Even then, the Pakistani state has tried to endure the militant backlash to protect its long-term regional objectives, through a unique mixture of security operations and accommodations, some formal and others informal.[27]

Manhunts in the tribal territories and 'live and let live' deals (2001–2006)

Ties between Pakistan's Inter-Services Intelligence (ISI) and Islamist militants are close, forged during the mujahideen's war against the Soviet occupation of Afghanistan in the 1980s, and in the insurgency in Indian-administered Kashmir in the 1990s. After 9/11, the US coerced Pakistan to agree to stop using Islamist militants as proxies. Musharraf received a threat from the US to sever support for the Taliban or be treated like the Taliban.[28] For Pakistan, the dangers of US military pressure were acute, given Bush's threats to attack states that harboured terrorists. But Pakistan would continue to apply its own logic in choosing which Islamist militants to engage, and how to engage them.

Pakistan proceeded to diagnose the solution to the problem as rooting out so-called 'foreign fighters' who were seeking refuge with Pashtun tribes along the Afghan border. This area was nominally governed as the Federally Administered Tribal Areas (FATA). The FATA was a relic of the pre-1947 British colonial era. The independently minded Pashtuns were exempt from Pakistan's national laws, but the state could collectively punish tribes for transgressions they committed, using locally recruited Frontier Corps paramilitaries. The regular army was supposed to keep out of the FATA. After 9/11, Pakistan broke with this arrangement and deployed the army's XI Corps, under Lieutenant-General Ali Jan Aurakzai. According to Aurakzai, the same coercive threat that the US made to Musharraf after 9/11 was now reiterated to the tribes:

> We explained to them that if we, the Pakistan Army, doesn't come into this area and secure the borders ... these undesirable elements will come here and make their sanctuaries and safe havens and this might provide justification to US coalition forces to conduct 'hot pursuit' operations in order to apprehend these people. There may even be aerial bombing and this entire area will be devastated.[29]

This approach began to falter as manhunts and blockades enraged the tribes. The army also had to contend with impenetrable mountain terrain, which helped to shield their quarry. Sometimes, targets were pursued to specific hideouts, as in an operation in March 2004 in Kalosha, South Waziristan. Frontier Corps and regular soldiers attacked compounds in Kalosha, understood to house foreign fighters who were being sheltered by a local tribal leader, Nek Mohammad. A battle ensued and well-entrenched militants inflicted dozens of casualties on Pakistan's security forces.[30]

Pakistan was in the throes of an insurgency that neither it nor the militants wanted. At this stage the militants remained fixated on the jihad in Afghanistan. The notion of certain fighters being explicitly foreign was problematic, given that Pashtuns travelled freely over the Afghanistan–Pakistan border. That said, internationally focused groups such as al-Qaeda were active in Pakistan, as bin Laden and others fled from the US occupation of Afghanistan. Just as mujahideen from around the world had flocked to the area to fight the USSR, some of them marrying into Pashtun tribes, now militants from the Persian Gulf, Central Asia and elsewhere were finding their way to the FATA. The US expected that Pakistani security forces would open up a second front against militant sanctuaries in the FATA, as NATO forces fought the Taliban in Afghanistan. Despite the sums of US money Pakistan was receiving in military aid, and in reward for those terrorists that it had captured or killed, the Pakistani government came to a different conclusion.

Pakistan's attention switched to how the army could extricate itself from the FATA. It is likely that Pakistan's military came to this conclusion at least in part because of a flaring of tension with India. From late 2001 it was involved in a huge military stand-off with Indian forces, provoked by an attack in Srinagar, Kashmir, which India attributed to Pakistani-backed proxies. This drew Pakistan's military east. And in the southwest, Pakistan was contending with the Baluchistan Liberation Army, which had renewed its secessionist struggle. The FATA in the northwest was just one theatre of Pakistani military concern.

Accommodation with the militants therefore made sense. Accommodation was also something of a default strategy for Pakistan: the state could restore the autonomy it had historically granted the ethnic Pashtun tribes, and it could fall back on the history of mutual benefit with Islamist militants from the era of proxy war in the 1980s. To Western audiences, Musharraf would portray deal-making with the militants as a means to exploit the divisions among them:

> My strategy was to wean away the Pashtun from the Taliban. I used *jirga*, a very tribal method to wean them away … All Taliban are Pashtun, but not all Pashtun are Taliban. You don't really know which ones are Taliban or not. Even if we got fifty percent [in a deal], I said to the US that this fifty percent are now against the others.[31]

Pakistan would make deals with different groups of militants at different times. Given that they had no identifiable single leadership structure, and since there was no monitoring to detect if the militants were reneging on the deals, what resulted were just local ceasefires.

In April 2004 Pakistan agreed to the Shakai deal with Nek Mohammad. In a public address, XI Corps commander Safdar Hussain addressed the tribes in brotherly terms, asking them to stop infiltrating Afghanistan. But they did not, and clashes with Pakistani forces resumed. In February 2005, a deal was struck in North Waziristan with a militant leader named Baitullah Mehsud, who also agreed to cease fighting in Afghanistan. He too reneged, and later formed Tehrik-e-Taliban Pakistan (TTP), an amalgam of Taliban factions that dedicatedly fought Pakistani forces. The capstone of Musharraf's deal-making strategy was the September 2006 North Waziristan Agreement, for which Aurakzai was tasked with restoring the old status quo that had existed with the tribes. This was not possible, since the Taliban were now slaughtering the very tribal leaders on whom the state was relying to implement the deal.

Pakistan was further tainted as an appeaser of the Taliban by the US. After the 2006 deal, NATO presented statistics of rising infiltration by fighters crossing from Pakistan into Afghanistan.[32] To the US it looked as if Pakistan was safeguarding the Taliban, whether by design or incompetence. This encouraged the US to take matters into its own hands by increasing its use of armed aerial drones to bomb militants on the Pakistani side of the border with Afghanistan. Aurakzai made Pakistan's perspective clear:

> Our friends in USA were bitterly opposed to peace agreements. Their oft-repeated argument was 'we don't pay you dollars to make peace agreements with

militants. We want you to fight and destroy them.'
As if US troops had made resounding successes in
their military operations in Afghanistan. The killing
of Nek Mohammad through [a] drone strike in South
Waziristan in May 2004 after he signed the Shakai
Deal with the government, further proves that US was
opposed to such deals. The North Waziristan agreement was a start to control the ever-growing militancy
in the region. We lost that opportunity.[33]

US drones were scoring tactical successes but, from a Pakistani
perspective, they were undoing progress in containing the
levels of conflict in Pakistan. The beneficiaries were the militants – they could exploit the mutually undermining nature
of US and Pakistani approaches and carry on their war in
Afghanistan.

In the FATA, alliances were fluid, just as they had been
in the British era. An age-old 'tribal tradition of alternating
between rebellion and participation in government, depending
on circumstances'[34] was repeating itself. Pakistan was trying to
avoid a wider war on its own territory. This war came anyway,
as a sharp escalation in the violence shook the Pakistani government out of its complacency.

Responding to an escalating war by fighting and talking (2007–2012)

Pakistan had been fighting a war confined to its remote and
underdeveloped northwest, at arm's length from the country's
heartland. This changed in July 2007 when Pakistani soldiers
assaulted Islamabad's Lal Masjid (Red Mosque), after a siege by
renegade clerics who refused to abide by the writ of the state. The
Lal Masjid clerics had found common cause with the FATA militants – to resist Pakistan's unholy alliance with the US. In the 1980s,

Pakistan's military had used Lal Masjid as a conduit to reach the Kashmiri-focused militants. Now, Pakistan was at odds with the very networks on which it had relied. Musharraf ordered soldiers to attack the mosque. Room-to-room fighting ensued and more than 100 people were killed in the resulting violence.

By ordering the assault, Musharraf hoped that decisive action would deter other Islamist militants. It had the opposite effect. The Lal Masjid assault and the rising number of US drone strikes in the FATA acted as rallying cries that galvanised Islamist militants to wage war on Pakistan.[35] The conflict now escalated along several dimensions. Militant groups in the FATA consolidated themselves under the TTP banner. Led by Baitullah Mehsud, the TTP allied with disgruntled Kashmir-focused groups to launch a countrywide suicide-bombing campaign. The TTP expanded its territorial presence, too, moving into neighbouring 'settled' (as opposed to tribal) areas such as the Swat valley.

Facing a situation that was slipping out of its control, Pakistan's strategy became a matter of prioritisation. Against those militants it deemed a mortal threat to its national interests, the military launched operations with a level of commitment hitherto unseen. Territory lost to the TTP would be encircled and bombed in an attempt to displace and trap the militants. According to Brigadier (Retd) Shaukat Qadir:

> The Taliban are divided amongst a number of factions but only two or three have taken up the call to wage war against the Pakistani state: Mullah Fazlullah's faction in Swat; Baitullah Mehsud's faction in South Waziristan; splinter groups in Punjab … Pakistan attacks South Waziristan because it perceives a threat as coming from there. It does not attack North Waziristan because it is not threatened from there.

Why should Pakistan fight against those that are not fighting against it?[36]

This strategic logic persisted even after Musharraf had left the scene. Having precipitated a domestic political crisis after trying to oust the chief justice of Pakistan, Musharraf gradually relinquished power.[37] He named General Ashfaq Kayani his successor as chief of the army staff. In 2008 Musharraf also relinquished the presidency, under pressure from a lawyers' movement that was protesting against his rule. Pakistan's new president would be Asif Ali Zardari (2008–13).

This new leadership inherited a dire situation. The TTP was occupying territory ever closer to Islamabad. The Swat valley fell to the militants in 2007. Retaking Swat was imperative, but it took the military several attempts. The army mounted *Operation Rah-e-Haq* ('Path to Truth') in three phases in 2007, 2008 and 2009.[38] These operations only temporarily displaced the militants. Kayani expressed his frustration to US General David Petraeus, who commiserated, saying that, as the US had found in Iraq, sometimes the same ground needed to be retaken repeatedly from insurgents.[39] It was not until May 2009, and *Operation Rah-e-Rast* ('The Right Way'), that Swat was recaptured.

Crucially, deals were still being used as enablers for these operations. In February 2009 the Malakand Accord was signed – a deal approved of by Kayani because it bought him time to husband his forces, telling US government interlocutors that he lacked the forces to fight on multiple fronts.[40] The Malakand Accord was proposed by the North West Frontier Province (NWFP) government, which had civilian authority over the Swat valley. NWFP authorities had tried to stave off the need for a military operation by freeing incarcerated militant Sufi Muhammed, to use him as a conduit to bargain with TTP-affiliated militants who were occupying Swat under Mullah Fazlullah.[41] The Malakand Accord allowed Kayani to prepare his forces and organise a mass evacuation of civilians out of Swat into refugee camps set up by the authorities, to clear a path for the army.[42]

After Swat, Pakistani attention turned to South Waziristan. Pakistan was suffering a growing number of suicide bombs right across the country. Suicide bombing was, geographically speaking, the forward-most projection of power that the militants could orchestrate, relying on countrywide networks to recruit, train and deploy suicide bombers. Many of the suicide bombers could be traced back to South Waziristan, and Baitullah Mehsud had to be confronted. To the Pakistani public, Zardari was keen to play down the sense that the army was acting at US behest. Behind the scenes Zardari had asked the US to expand its drone attacks beyond al-Qaeda and Afghan Taliban to include the TTP.[43] A US drone killed Baitullah Mehsud in August 2009. He was replaced by Hakimullah Mehsud, who came from the same tribe, just before the start of the Pakistani military's *Operation Rah-e-Nijat* ('Path to Deliverance') in October 2009.[44] Hakimullah Mehsud, too, was killed by a drone strike in November 2013.

Despite its fight with the TTP, Pakistan was keen not to provoke the ire of every Islamist armed group in its midst. Resisting US pressure at this time, Pakistan held back from attacking the Afghan-focused militants of the Haqqani network in North Waziristan (although the network came under US drone attack). Similarly, Pakistan did not attack the so-called Quetta Shura, which the US had identified as the Baluchistan-based hub of Afghan insurgent activity.

Another case in point was LeT, which did not join with the TTP to wage war on Pakistan. LeT conducted the November 2008 attack in Mumbai, India, in which a team of gunmen set off from Pakistan by boat to attack India's financial capital, killing 164 people, including civilians and Indian police (nine of the ten attackers were also killed). This brazen attack risked provoking another Indo-Pakistani conflict. Indian restraint after this attack hinged on assurances by Pakistan that it would crack down on LeT. However, LeT leader Hafiz Saeed went on to set up Jamaat-ud-Dawa, a non-militant front for LeT. Pakistan jailed LeT commander Zakiur Rehman Lakhvi, but according to Indian sources he was communicating with LeT by mobile phone from inside Adiala jail. Regardless of how loudly India or the West might complain, Pakistan calculated that tolerating groups such as LeT carried less risk than waging war on them.[45]

The gravest Pakistani concern was that the insurgency would envelop Punjab, the heartland of the state. The TTP drew on militant groups that were already rooted in Punjab, and that had previously fought in Kashmir. These included groups such as Jaish-e-Mohammed (JeM), an anti-Indian group, and Sipah-e-Sahaba Pakistan (SSP), a sectarian Sunni group involved in targeting Pakistan's Shia minority. The convergence of Islamist militants could be as mercurial as it was ideological, with the TTP sometimes paying for the services of JeM and SSP to expand its reach across Pakistan.[46] In sum, Pakistan's brinkmanship strategy, which blended security operations and accommodation, remained in place.

No binary choice between talks and war (2013–2014)

Pakistan is a state made fragile by the sheer breadth of the complexities that it faces. The militancy Pakistan suffers has thrived on its weaknesses. Poverty, illiteracy and ethno-religious fault lines are rife among a burgeoning population of 180 million. Pakistan's rulers have struggled to contend with these challenges, preoccupied by coups staged by an army that has directly ruled Pakistan for 33 years of its existence following coups in 1958, 1977 and 1999, and bruising battles between venal politicians. Moreover, despite being called the Islamic Republic of Pakistan, religion has occupied an ill-defined position within the state, leading to sectarian strife. Pakistan's military has arguably made the situation worse, using the narrative of jihad, and the threat of Hindu subjugation of Muslims, to mobilise the very armed groups that, after 9/11, the US was telling it to confront.[47] To address the root causes of the conflict with Islamist militants, the focus must also turn to the battle of ideas in Pakistan over extremist Islam, to Pakistan's structural frailties of regionalism and poverty, and to its pervading sense of regional insecurity. Fighting and talking just buys time for the Pakistan state to crisis-manage the problem. It allows Pakistan's military to safeguard its influence within the state, and with international partners such as the US.

During the presidential election campaign in 2013, how to deal with the TTP became the subject of national debate. Former cricketer Imran Kahn campaigned on a platform that responded to widespread anger over how US drone strikes breached Pakistan's sovereignty. He advocated talks with the TTP instead, and even tried to march peacefully into the tribal areas. When Hakimullah Mehsud was killed in the US drone strike, some in Pakistan reacted with outrage that prospects for peace talks had also died.

While it is tempting to simplify Pakistan's policy options as a binary choice between war and peace, the circumstances since 2001 belie a more complex reality. Imran Kahn lost the election to Nawaz Sharif, who, with Army Chief of Staff Raheel Sharif, has faced the question of what do about the TTP. Hopes for a full-blown peace process with the TTP seem misconstrued, however, not least because of a lack of will. Pakistan's army does not support peace talks with the TTP, and it is likely that Pakistan's awkward coexistence with Islamist armed groups will persist.

After 9/11, Pakistan dug in for the long haul. The one strategic goal that it achieved was to stave off a US military escalation, based on the notion of Pakistan being a state sponsor of terrorism. Moreover, Pakistan has still received around US$20 billion in US aid since 2002.[48] The deaths and public ignominy resulting from US drone strikes in Pakistan, and the US Navy SEAL raid in Abbottabad to kill bin Laden in May 2011, highlight the ambiguity of this outcome. But these raids are a relatively small price to pay when considering the anger the US has felt over Pakistan's inconsistent fight with Islamist militants. With NATO drawing down its presence in Afghanistan since 2014, Pakistan has retained the role perhaps not of kingmaker in Kabul, but certainly of having an abiding influence in the affairs of its neighbour.

Years after his presidency, when asked to reflect on the policy of deal-making with Taliban factions, Musharraf could not help but reflect on Pakistan having been far quicker to grasp the need for a political solution involving the Taliban than the US-led coalition in Afghanistan had been: 'Even if we failed in 2002 and 2004 to make a deal with the Taliban, even now you have to bring the Pashtun into a deal. We should find which group is for peace and use it against the others in Pakistan and Afghanistan.'[49] As is explored in the next chapter, eventually even NATO has swung closer to this interpretation.

Do these policies arise from cunning or desperation?

Ultimately, the policy question addressed in this chapter has been: which armed groups is it possible to work with and which will be deemed irreconcilable? In making such choices, a state's values, its objectives and its sheer level of desperation are likely to be factors. The matter of desperation is an important one on which to close. No matter how Machiavellian leaders such as Putin and Musharraf may appear to be, armed groups that stubbornly and brutally refuse to be subdued are a real predicament for states.

In particular, armed groups that fuse local grievances with Islamist ideologies present especially tough challenges. Policymakers may feel they have few good options against constellations of militants that operate alternately as diffuse terror networks and ground-holding insurgencies, and that are bound by a powerful, transcendental ideology that justifies their war. Facing such a challenge, states might opt for a divide-and-rule policy response, pragmatically choosing which armed groups to confront. Splitting the opposition may only put off having to deal with the root causes of the violence, and may compound the problem for future generations. But some degree of selection – of deciding which kinds of armed groups to work with, and which ones to vilify – remains not only the choice of the cunning, but also the choice of the desperate.

States may conceal their true strategic intent, as Pakistan has done, mixing fighting and talking. To achieve deception, states may present their actions as accommodating some armed groups, but use this to mask a more genuine desire to seek their elimination. The inverse can also be true, of seeming to use force to destroy armed groups, but only weakening them to allow their survival. Splitting the opposition can be a viable approach to weakening secessionists, as in Russia. In each case, alliances have been fluid, and have relied on cutting deals and coming to arrangements with some armed groups while the fighting rages on.

Notes

1   Pervez Musharraf, *In the Line of Fire: A Memoir* (London: Simon & Schuster, 2006), p. 332.
2   BBC News, 'Putin Reject's "Child Killer" Talks', BBC, 7 September 2004, http://news.bbc.co.uk/2/hi/europe/3633668.stm.
3   'Chechen Official Puts Death Toll for Two Wars at up to 160,000', *New York Times*, 16 August 2005.
4   Roland Dannreuther and Luke March, 'Chechnya: Has Moscow Won?', *Survival: Global Politics and Strategy*, vol. 50, no. 4, August 2008.
5   Lev Nikolayevich Tolstoy, *Hadji Murad* (New York: Random House Vintage Books, 2012).
6   Anatol Lieven, *Chechnya: Tombstone of Russian Power* (New Haven, CT: Yale University Press, 1999), p. 23.
7   Gordon M. Hahn, *Russia's Islamic Threat* (New Haven, CT: Yale University Press, 2007), pp. 30–2.
8   International Crisis Group, 'The North Caucasus: The Challenges of Integration (I), Ethnicity and Conflict', Europe Report No. 220 (19 October 2012), pp. 9–10.
9   Sebastian Smith, *Allah's Mountains: The Battle for Chechnya* (London: Tauris, 2006); Lieven, *Chechnya: Tombstone of Russian Power*, pp. 269–300.
10 Dannreuther and March, 'Chechnya: Has Moscow Won?'.
11 James Hughes, *Chechnya: From Nationalism to Jihad* (Philadelphia, PA: University of Pennsylvania Press, 2007) of Pennsylvania Press), p. xii; Hahn, *Russia's Islamic Threat*, pp. 31, 40.
12 Hughes, *Chechnya: From Nationalism to Jihad*, p. xiii; Anatol Lieven, 'Islamist Anger Feeds on Chechnya History', *Financial Times*, 19 April 2013; International Crisis Group, 'The North Caucasus', p. 11.
13 Alexander Litvinenko and Yuri Felshtinsky, *Blowing up Russia: the Return of the KGB* (New York: Encounter Books, 2007), pp. 1–20, 100–47.
14 'No Let-Up in Chechnya: Russia is Winning Territory in its Secessionist Republic, but Little Else', *The Economist*, 17 February 2000; International Crisis Group, 'The North Caucasus', pp. 11–12.
15 Hahn, *Russia's Islamic Threat*, pp. 24–5; Smith, *Allah's Mountains*, p. 78; Domitilla Sagramoso, 'The Radicalisation of Islamic Salafi Jamaats in the North Caucasus: Moving Closer to the Global Jihadist Movement?', *Europe Asia Studies*, vol. 64, no. 3, May 2012, pp. 561–95.
16 International Crisis Group, 'The North Caucasus', p. 13.
17 Smith, *Allah's Mountains*, p. xxiv.
18 Fiona Hill and Clifford Gaddy, *Mr Putin: Operative in the Kremlin* (Washington DC: Brookings Institution, 2013), p. 244.
19 'Chechnya's War Hangover: Russian Troop Withdrawal Does Not Equal Peace', IISS *Strategic Comments* 5, 4 June 2009.
20 'Islamists in Russia', *The Economist*, 27 April 2013.
21 International Crisis Groups, 'North Caucasus', pp. 1–16.
22 John Russell, *Chechnya – Russia's 'War on Terror'* (London/New York: Routledge, 2007), p. 6 and chapter 8.
23 Hahn, *Russia's Islamic Threat*, pp. 6–19.

[24] International Crisis Groups, 'North Caucasus', p. 33.

[25] Seth Jones, 'Pakistan's Dangerous Game', *Survival: Global Politics and Strategy*, vol. 49, no. 1, Spring 2007; Ashley Tellis, 'Pakistan – Conflicted Ally in the War on Terror', Carnegie Endowment for International Peace, Policy Brief 56, December 2007; Ahmed Rashid, *Descent into Chaos: The US and the Failure of Nation Building in Pakistan, Afghanistan, and Central Asia* (New York: Viking Penguin, 2008).

[26] Estimate from all armed group violence: http://www.satp.org.

[27] This argument is fully developed in Samir Puri, *Pakistan's War on Terrorism: Strategies for Engaging Jihadist Armed Groups since 9/11* (New York: Routledge, 2011).

[28] Bob Woodward, *Bush at War* (London: Simon & Schuster, 2003), pp. 47, 58–9; Musharraf, *In the Line of Fire*, pp. 201–7.

[29] Lt.-Gen. (Retd) Ali Jan Aurakzai, undated interview: 'Pakistan's War on Terror', DVD, produced by Maj.-Gen. Shaukut Sultan, Director General, Inter-Services Public Relations, Pakistan. Also available on http://www.ispr.gov.pk.

[30] Hilary Synnott, *Transforming Pakistan: Ways out of Instability*, Adelphi Paper 406 (London: IISS, 2009); C. Christine Fair and Seth Jones, 'Pakistan's War Within', *Survival: Global Politics and Strategy*, vol. 51, no. 6, December 2009–January 2010.

[31] Musharraf, address to Cambridge Union, Cambridge, UK, 13 June 2011.

[32] 'Taliban Attacks Double After Pakistan's Deal with Militants', *Guardian*, 29 September 2006.

[33] Interview, Lt-Gen. (Retd) Aurakzai, Islamabad (by email), February–March 2011.

[34] Lieven, *Pakistan: A Hard Country* (New York: Public Affairs, 2011), p. 349; Joshua T. White, *Islamic Politics and US Policy in Pakistan's North-West Frontier* (Arlington, VA: Center on Faith & International Affairs at the Institute for Global Engagement, 2008), p. 132.

[35] Manjeet S. Pardesi, 'The Battle for the Soul of Pakistan at Islamabad's Red Mosque', in C. Christine Fair and Sumit Ganguly (eds), *Treading on Hallowed Ground: Counterinsurgency Operations in Sacred Spaces* (Oxford: Oxford University Press, 2008), pp. 97–107; '12 Dead as Lal Masjid Students Provoke gunfight' and 'Curfew Around Lal Masjid as Operation Approved', *Daily Times*, 4 July 2007; '1,200 Surrender at Lal Masjid' and 'Chief Cleric Held, Asked to Order Surrender', *Daily Times*, 5 July 2007.

[36] Interview with Brig. (Retd) Shaukat Qadir, Islamabad (by telephone), 22 March 2011.

[37] Chief Justice Iftikhar Chaudhry (2005–13) had attempted to block Musharraf from seeking re-election as president while remaining chief of staff. Musharraf suspended him in March 2007, a move that provoked mass protests by lawyers. In a climbdown, Musharraf was forced to reinstate Chaudhry in July 2007.

[38] Syed Zaidi, 'Pakistan's Anti-Taliban Counter-Insurgency', *RUSI Journal*, vol. 155, no. 1, February 2010.

[39] 'CENTCOM Gen. Petraeus Meets with Pakistani COAS Kiyani', US State Department Cable, authored

24 January 2009, released by Wikileaks 30 November 2010 as 09ISLAMABAD155.

40 'Scenesetter for Gen. Kiyani's Visit to Washington', US State Department Cable, authored 19 February 2009, released by Wikileaks 30 November 2010 as 09ISLAMABAD365.

41 Full text of the Malakand Accord, the 'Nizam-e-Adl Regulation 2009': http://www.satp.org/satporgtp/countries/pakistan/document/papers/Nizam-e-AdlRegulation2009.htm.

42 See articles in Islamabad's *Daily Times*: 'More Peace Deals with Militants in the Pipeline: NWFP Law Minister', 23 April 2008; 'TTP Says Osama Welcome in Swat: Taliban Reject Peace Accord', 22 April 2009; 'Armed Taliban Back on Mingora Roads: TNSM Rejects Darul Qaza', 4 May 2009; 'Human Exodus and War Against Taliban' and '69 Taliban Killed, Forces Seize Swat Emerald Mine', 7 May 2009; 'Editorial: Pakistan Goes to War in Swat', 9 May 2009.

43 Bob Woodward, *Obama's Wars: The Inside Story* (London: Simon & Schuster, 2010), pp. 26, 11, 71.

44 'The Pakistani Taliban: Falling Out', *The Economist*, 29 August 2009.

45 '26/11 Accused Lakhvi Communicating With LeT Cadres From Prison: Intel', *Times of India*, 25 October 2011; Stephen Tankel, *Storming the World Stage: the Story of LeT* (London: Hurst, 2011).

46 'Terrorists Increase Activity in Advance of Waziristan Operation', US State Department Cable, authored 16 October 2009, released 30 November 2010, 09ISLAMABAD2523.

47 On how Pakistan's root fragilities have contributed to its armed-group challenge, see Farzana Shaikh, *Making Sense of Pakistan* (London: Hurst & Company, 2009).

48 Susan B. Epsteim and K. Alan Kronstadt, 'Pakistan: US Foreign Assistance', US Congressional Research Service, 1 July 2013.

49 Musharraf address to Cambridge Union.

CHAPTER FOUR

When partnerships of states confront armed groups

If I say I want protection for Mullah Omar [to enable talks] the international community has two choices. Remove me or leave, if they disagree. If I am removed in the cause of peace for Afghanistan by force by them, then I will be very happy ... But we are not at that stage yet.

Hamid Karzai, 2008[1]

The US has had trouble agreeing to a concrete timetable for withdrawal because they feel it would appear tantamount to an admission of defeat. But that isn't the case ... it is not evidence of a defeat, but of a victory, of a severe blow we have inflicted on al-Qaeda and the militias.

Nouri al-Maliki, 2008[2]

This chapter presents a very different manifestation of the strategic conundrum of confronting armed groups. In Afghanistan and Iraq, US-led coalitions intervened to change regimes, before handing power to reconstituted host governments. In both cases bitter wars ensued with groups that remained outside the state-building process. Ownership over the strategy to deal with these groups changed over time. At first, foreign forces owned the problem. Later, it became the preserve of the Afghan and Iraqi governments, albeit bolstered by foreign firepower. During this transition the strategic calculus of local governments would diverge notably from the foreign interveners over how to deal with the armed-group threat.

The notion of shared, possibly disputed ownership over strategy remains important today. Even if one concludes that both of these US-led state-building endeavours were exercises in hubris that reflected a post-9/11 fervour, and hence were mistakes never to be repeated, they still contain valuable insights. Although large-scale Western interventions are much less viable policy options, there is now a greater emphasis on bolstering local forces with selective Western support. It is the recipients of this assistance – not the West – that put their boots on the ground.

As previous chapters have shown, dealing with an insurgency at home is a complex matter, even if it involves a single and largely unified armed group. The complexities only multiply if several states act in an ad hoc alliance, or under the auspices of a multilateral body, to assist a host government that has its own ideas. With so many actors and interests, harmonising the various tracks of engagement towards a purposeful goal may not be realistic. And yet, the most fundamental strategic choices still revolve around war and political processes, compromise or conflict. The Afghan and Iraqi wars illustrate how a policy mix is managed and mismanaged when many governments are involved – and how only illusory progress against armed groups may result.

Afghanistan: neither defeating nor reconciling with the Taliban

The US deemed that al-Qaeda, a terrorist group with a pan-Islamist and anti-Western ideology, had been helped in carrying out the 9/11 attacks by the Taliban, a ruthlessly puritanical but essentially local movement. The US proceeded to fight and marginalise the Taliban. But the Taliban, which comprised several autonomous factions, ensured its survivability by operating across the border with Pakistan. Achieving only military deadlock after a decade of war, the US, its NATO allies and the Afghan government instead began to try to reconcile with the Taliban.

Much has been written about how Western governments tied themselves in knots in Afghanistan.[3] Their intervention was bedevilled by its multiplicity of over-ambitious goals: counter-terrorism against al-Qaeda; counter-insurgency against the Taliban; building democracy in Kabul; administering vast amounts of economic assistance; and weaning Afghanistan off dependence on opium production. Over time, these goals suffered from strategic drift. Absent was a coherent strategic vision to guide intervening international countries in deciding which of their many goals had predominance. Security and state-building were pursued as conjoined aims, each seen as a precursor to the other, as the drawdown of NATO forces in 2014 loomed ever closer.

It is more instructive to ask where the Afghans fit into all of this. Successive Afghan governments under the presidencies of Hamid Karzai (interim president from 2001, president 2004–14) and Ashraf Ghani (2014–) saw the Taliban threat differently to their foreign backers. The Afghan state and NATO members grappled with the question of fighting or talking to the Taliban, as did regional powers such as Pakistan. Each had a different answer. A lack of strategic unity was to be expected. But, as US relations with Karzai moved from favour in 2001 to disfavour by the time of his exit in 2014, the rift was so substantial that strategy towards the Taliban was not being forged in partnership with, but being foisted on, the Afghan government.

Regime change, state-building and Taliban renewal (2001–2008)

The style of violence associated with the Taliban movement, first as abettors and later as purveyors of mass-casualty suicide attacks, would understandably make it difficult for Western states to see the movement as a legitimate political force. That they would ever need to was lost in the haze of outrage after 9/11. Bush was categorical in his aims. 'These demands are not open to negotiation or discussion. The Taliban must act and act immediately. They will hand over the terrorists or they will share in their fate.'[4]

The 2001 US intervention tipped the scales in an Afghan civil war that had raged for years between factions of the former mujahideen, which had fought against the Soviet 1979–89 Afghan occupation. The US and Pakistan backed the mujahideen in this war, but US interest waned after the Soviet withdrawal. Afghanistan then descended into civil war. Pakistan backed the mujahideen factions it felt were most pliant towards its interests. It supported the Taliban, which mainly comprised Pashtuns, a people living across the porous, mountainous Afghanistan–Pakistan border. Pakistan helped the Taliban beat the Northern Alliance, a conglomerate of ethnically Tajik, Uzbek and Hazara warlords. In 1996, the Taliban seized Kabul and proceeded to impose a puritanical vision of Islam on Afghanistan.[5]

The US military intervention after 9/11 reversed this outcome, backing the Northern Alliance to rout the Taliban. Foreign states took responsibility for Afghan reconstruction at the December 2001 Bonn Conference. To govern Afghanistan, an interim council was established, with Karzai at its head. The International Security Assistance Force (ISAF) was established, made up of NATO militaries, with the goals of training a new Afghan army, stabilising the country and being guarantors of Karzai's regime during the state-building process. The international mandate was strong, since ISAF and Bonn both received UN Security Council backing.

The Taliban, however, had not been destroyed. Nor was it involved in post-war arrangements. There simply was no Western will at this time to deal with an enemy implicated in the 9/11 attacks. As former ambassador James Dobbins, US representative to the Northern Alliance in 2001, later reflected:

> Within a few weeks, the Taliban had been routed, and a moderate, broadly based, and representative government installed in its place. Unfortunately, this deceptively easy initial success emboldened American policymakers. Before Afghanistan's reconstruction had begun, the Bush administration's attention shifted to the next campaign in its 'global war on terror'. Afghanistan … would be the most poorly resourced American venture into nation building in more than sixty years.[6]

As he also recalls, regional diplomacy failed to adequately involve key local powers with a stake in Afghanistan. India and Iran had supported the Northern Alliance, but at Bonn, Iran's cooperation was not sought by the US.[7]

Crucially, Pakistan's security calculus remained fixed on tacitly backing the Taliban. Indeed, the Taliban's survival was guaranteed by its ability to retreat to Pakistan after its 2001 rout. The original Kandahar-centred Taliban, led by Mullah Omar, fled to Quetta. The Haqqani network, led by Jalaluddin and his son Sirajuddin, based itself in Pakistan's tribal Waziristan agencies. Alongside other groups under warlords, such as Gulbuddin Hekmatyar's Hizb-e-Islami, the Taliban movement was in effect a collection of factions. Operating across the Afghanistan–Pakistan border, it could wage a prolonged campaign against NATO and Karzai's government.[8]

The Afghan political process was drifting apart from progress on security. Karzai, elected president in October 2004, was dubbed the 'mayor of Kabul' due to his reliance on the warlords of the Northern Alliance. US defence secretary Donald Rumsfeld's 'light footprint', and his aversion to a large peacekeeping force outside major cities, meant that Karzai's government could not expand its control beyond Kabul.[9] The onset of the Iraq War had shifted US focus, and by June 2007, it had 27,000 military personnel in Afghanistan and 155,000 in Iraq.

Nevertheless Karzai kept faith, telling the US that NATO 'needs to complete the win' over the Taliban.[10] The NATO mission eventually expanded right across Afghanistan during 2006. As it did so, the Taliban retaliated robustly in the eastern and southern regions in which the movement was rooted. One such province was Helmand, where British forces struggled to create space for development work to take root. To secure Musa Qala, Helmand's district centre, British forces alternated between fighting and talking to tribal elders. The elders sought assurances that neither British nor Taliban forces would take the city. A 'live and let live' deal was reached in September 2006 that allowed British forces to leave. This deal collapsed in February 2007 when the Taliban reoccupied the city. In December 2007, NATO and Afghan National Army (ANA) forces retook Musa Qala.[11] These events illustrated how hard it could prove to establish an enduring NATO and ANA presence in Taliban-controlled regions.

Each NATO contingent was assigned a province to stabilise. Some NATO countries limited the rules of engagement by which their forces operated to avoid combat roles. With the insurgency showing no signs of abating, political will in some NATO countries faltered under domestic pressure over a seemingly open-ended military commitment. Over time, Canada, Germany, France, the Netherlands and others reduced their ISAF contributions, patrolling only safer areas, limiting their roles to non-combat-oriented tasks, such as training the ANA and Afghan police. The US remained the largest contributor to ISAF, but as Bush's presidency entered its final year in 2008, it remained primarily embroiled in Iraq.

By now the Taliban had regained its footing, restoring command and logistics arrangements in southern and eastern Afghanistan, and linking these to its Pakistani sanctuaries.[12] As the Taliban insurgency evolved, it defied simple characterisation as an exclusively nationalist, regional or religious movement. It was each of these things. Rooted in Pashtun ethnic identity, in a traditional vision of Islam and in a shared history of fighting foreign occupiers, the Taliban remained a fiercely independent movement, albeit finding common cause with international jihadists and adopting their suicide-bombing tactics.[13]

Karzai was trapped between the Taliban's resurgent threat and his overbearing – but under-resourced – foreign backers. Venality reigned as Karzai focused on building patronage networks to embed his rule.[14] Crucially, Karzai began to think flexibly about the Taliban. A leaked 2008 US cable for secretary of defense Robert Gates judged that: 'Karzai's senior-level Taliban reconciliation initiative is more about strengthening his political base and his relationship with the Saudis than anything else.'[15] Kabul was moving at a different speed in thinking about reconciliation. The US still had a long road to travel before deciding reconciliation was its policy – a road that involved military escalation, and a deterioration of relations with Karzai.

Whose policy mix? The interplay between counter-insurgency, counter-terrorism and reconciliation (2009–2013)

President Barack Obama took office in January 2009 and requested a review of US 'Af-Pak' strategy. After consulting his experts Obama chose to deploy 30,000 extra soldiers, with the caveat that it would only be for one year. Moreover, this surge was below the 40,000 soldiers requested by General Stanley McChrystal. Obama's focus was on an eventual US withdrawal, not an open-ended commitment – this was a surge with a clear deadline.[16]

McChrystal was appointed to lead US forces in Afghanistan based on his record with Petraeus in Iraq in applying counter-insurgency (COIN) doctrine. In Afghanistan, COIN sought to clear, hold, build and transfer areas to ANA control. As the surge forces arrived, large operations were mounted in 2010 in Kandahar and Marja, inflicting reverses on the Taliban. However, there was a serious divergence with Karzai, who thought it a misdirection of force to take the war to the Afghan countryside.[17] Intelligence-led raids against mid-level Taliban figures, involving night raids on Afghan homes, also angered Karzai. Petraeus retorted that COIN and counter-terrorism were mutually supportive, and intelligence generated by good relations with the locals facilitated these raids.[18]

However, conflating the counter-terrorism and COIN missions would hamper the clarity with which the US articulated its security objectives. This conflation was rooted in assumptions made in 2001 that the link between al-Qaeda and the Taliban was symbiotic. Research by Felix Kuehn and

Alex Strick van Linschoten helps to disentangle this matter. While al-Qaeda and the Taliban would eventually be pushed together by the common cause of fighting NATO, initially 'the relationship was strained and generally extended no further than individual contacts ... al-Qaeda and the Afghan Taliban remain two distinct entities, with different member-ships, ideologies, objectives'.[19] Eventually, the Taliban came to resemble al-Qaeda, at least in using suicide attacks to strike even Kabul's most secure areas, chipping away at Karzai's regime and at NATO commitment with mass-casualty suicide-bomb and gun attacks. Fighting a 'war on terrorism' in Afghanistan had become a self-fulfilling prophecy.

Progress along the security track was ambiguous at best. While the surge had made progress, it was clear that 'the Taliban's resistance has left insurgents in control of enough territory to remain militarily viable',[20] according to analyst Stephen Biddle. General (Retd) Karl Eikenberry, US ambas-sador to Afghanistan between 2009 and 2011, was blunter: 'In short, COIN failed in Afghanistan.'[21] As the Taliban withstood the surge, the US reluctantly adjusted its policy to explore reconciliation, pursuing its COIN and counter-terrorism objec-tives concurrently.

The very term 'reconciliation' was loosely defined. It encom-passed grassroots attempts to demobilise low-ranking Taliban to try to fragment the movement from below. A grand bargain with Taliban leaders, and their Pakistani benefactors, was never spelled out as the goal. Instead, reconciliation haphazardly evolved to encompass top-down and bottom-up engagement. It did not help that the US accorded reconciliation a low prior-ity. In 2009, alongside his Af-Pak strategy review, Obama appointed diplomat Richard Holbrooke to coordinate the political aspects of US policy in the region. But, as Holbrooke's adviser Vali Nasr commented:

During the review, there was no discussion of diplomacy and a political settlement at all. A commitment to finding a political settlement to the war would have put diplomacy front and center and organized military and intelligence operations in Afghanistan to support it ... But the military thought talk of reconciliation undermined America's commitment to fully resourced COIN ... This imbalance at the heart of American foreign policy was Obama's to fix, the strategic review the place to do it.[22]

Diplomacy, as Holbrooke envisaged, required negotiations with the Taliban, and regional dialogue with India, Iran and Pakistan. For Holbrooke, the arrival of US surge forces was the best time to press for talks – it reflected the maximum pressure the US would exert on the Taliban. Conversely, Petraeus and Mike Mullen, the chairman of the joint chiefs of staff, wanted to implement COIN *before* broaching talks with the Taliban. McChrystal thought that military pressure would be vital in pushing Taliban members to switch sides, while prematurely drawing down US forces would be a mistake.[23] The lack of coordination was acute. Petraeus called Holbrooke his 'diplomatic wingman', and Holbrooke told his staff that Petraeus's 'job should be to drop the bombs when I tell him to'.[24] This was more than just a personality clash: it was the dilemma of managing concurrent approaches playing out. According to Nasr:

As we went from 'fight and talk' to 'talk while leaving' the prospect of a good outcome began to grow dimmer. The Taliban did not think that we were winning, they thought that *they* were winning. Talks were not about arranging their surrender, but about hastening our departure.[25]

Key figures in the US effort fell by the wayside. In July 2010 McChrystal, in an interview with *Rolling Stone*, so frankly expressed frustration with the wider US approach that he was relieved of his command.[26] In December 2010 Holbrooke died of a heart attack. It was not until February 2011 that Hillary Clinton, the secretary of state, formally endorsed reconciliation.[27] But, even then, it was clear that the United States' main focus was on fighting the Taliban.

The tentativeness of reconciliation efforts was partly a consequence of the practical difficulties of talking to the Taliban. The Taliban did not offer a central focal point to which talks could be directed. In 2010 Holbrooke and his German counterpart Bernd Mützelburg made contact with Tayeb Agha, a relative of Mullah Omar.[28] Through this channel Taliban leaders conveyed that they wanted to talk to the US before talking to Karzai's government. Karzai was worried – a deal made over his head would weaken his standing. Pakistan, too, was concerned at being marginalised by bilateral US–Taliban talks, and duly tried to control the freedom with which Taliban leaders in Pakistan could respond to overtures for talks.[29]

Parallel outreach efforts were taking place involving European and Gulf countries, each putting out feelers for Taliban willing to talk. Problems arose over who, precisely, could be understood as speaking on behalf of the Taliban. The Taliban relied on foreign volunteers, warlords and other go-betweens to function. Mapping the concentric circles of these power structures was no simple task.[30] To illustrate the confusion that could ensue, according to a story recounted by an official in Karzai's office, an imposter who claimed to be Mullah Mansour, a Taliban leader, duped the British Secret Intelligence Service (SIS) into flying him from Pakistan to Kabul for peace talks before he fled the scene, having taken considerable payment.[31]

The Afghan government attempted its own outreach. Karzai appointed Burhanuddin Rabbani, a leading former mujahideen figure and president from 1992–96, to head Afghanistan's High Peace Council. However, a suicide bomber killed Rabbani on 20 September 2011.[32] There were as many outreach efforts as governments involved. In 2012 Obama was explicit that 'we're pursuing a negotiated peace. In coordination with the Afghan government, my administration has been in direct discussions with the Taliban.'[33] The extent of this coordination was moot.

When, in 2013, the Taliban was granted a political office in Qatar, to formally announce its readiness for talks, Karzai was enraged by the impression that the Taliban was staging what resembled a triumphant embassy opening; he even suspended bilateral talks over the status of US forces after 2014. The Qatar office was closed before negotiations could begin. Reconciliation efforts, ad hoc as they were, came to focus on prompting low-level Taliban defections, and on facilitating the US withdrawal, rather than on searching for a settlement to end the war.[34]

Epilogue: greater Afghan ownership after the ISAF drawdown (2014)

It is easy to see the Afghan government as a passive player in a war effort run by the US and its NATO allies. Ultimately, the aim of the international effort was to empower the Afghan government; but, as its ownership increased, the government also inherited major security problems. The Afghan police, ANA and its intelligence agency, the National Directorate for Strategy, were feeling the strain in a war with the Taliban that had not abated.

The Taliban had pursued a 'wait and see' strategy over talks. As long as its fighters could rotate into Pakistan by crossing the border with Afghanistan, the insurgency persisted. As the ISAF military presence diminished, the Taliban knew that the balance of forces would swing into a more straightforward equation:

Taliban versus the ANA, with whatever residual foreign support that remained. Moreover, since Pakistan continued to have a stake in the movement, the extent to which the Taliban could even speak for itself in talks remained contestable. Ultimately, even if the Taliban eventually renounced armed struggle and was granted a political stake, the Afghan elite would be likely to resist any process that altered the balance of power between Kabul and wider regions.[35] These were the dilemmas awaiting Ghani, who replaced Karzai in September 2014.

In his book *Fixing Failed States*, Ghani wrote: 'we hope that Afghan leaders and their international partners can learn from the past and act with wisdom and determination'.[36] Afghans would be forgiven for being baffled at the poor progress their partners have made. State-building, COIN, counter-terrorism, reconciliation and counter-narcotics operations were pursued concurrently, but effective linkages were not forged between these endeavours. A circular logic was at play: security was needed for state-building, and state-building was needed to improve security. Neither was clearly enunciated as an end or means. It was simply too expansive an agenda.[37]

Outcomes were therefore ambiguous. Fighting the Taliban into a position of vulnerability proved hard, despite the considerable pressure NATO and the ANA exerted. Talking to the Taliban proved just as hard, given the atomised nature of the insurgency and Pakistan's role. In 15 years none of the war's protagonists had moved much closer to a situation that they might consider satisfactory, and perhaps least of all the Afghan government.

Iraq: as the armed-group challenge ends, another begins
By toppling Saddam Hussein's regime in 2003, the US-led coalition of occupying states fractured Iraq into a myriad of armed factions. The Coalition came to rely on a policy of legiti-

mising some armed groups and fighting others. The roots of this policy lay in the Coalition Provisional Authority (CPA), which governed Iraq immediately after the invasion. Given scant pre-war preparation for what might follow the invasion, the CPA scrambled to legitimise groups that had formerly been hostile to Saddam's regime, bringing Kurdish and some Shia groups into the new Iraqi state. Coalition forces excluded Sunni and other Shia from this process and deemed them insurgents. Years later some insurgent groups were engaged in dialogue, in increasingly desperate US attempts to stabilise Iraq. The new Iraqi state would in effect be cobbled together in this fashion, through a process of fighting and talking to various factions.

This strategy of selective legitimisation made a lasting impact, inadvertently bequeathing to Iraq a legacy of sectarian politics and violence that persisted after the departure of Coalition forces. This became all too apparent as Iraq yet again suffered sectarian infighting that presaged the rise of Islamic State, also known as ISIS or ISIL, in 2014, which in turn led to the return to limited US intervention to support the Iraqi state. The US blamed Iraq's new leaders for their sectarian stewardship. But it will be left to the reader's judgement whether the tactics employed by the Coalition after 2003 to contain Iraq's civil war relate at all to the outcomes of a decade hence, and whether a nuanced reading of events belies the simple narrative that Iraq was former prime minister Nouri al-Maliki's (2006–14) to lose.

Absorbing some groups into the state; excluding others (2003–2006)

Before the invasion, the Ba'athist regime had ruled Iraq uninterrupted since it took power in a coup in 1968. After Saddam Hussein (1979–2003), a key figure in the ruling Ba'ath Party, became president, his regime held Iraq's various ethno-religious factions in a brutal and artificial equilibrium. The Shia majority and the Kurds were repressed, granting the Sunni minority a dominance that was the basis of Ba'athist rule. This all came to an abrupt end following the toppling of the regime. US forces captured Baghdad in April 2003. Later that month the US established a governing body, later renamed the CPA, which would rule Iraq for one year. This was supposed to be a transition phase, preceding a handover of power to a new, popularly elected government.

A descent into chaos ensued. 'The US-led invasion of Iraq in 2003 had a traumatic effect on Iraqi society', reflected Emma Sky (an adviser to the US military in Iraq) and Safa Rasul al-Sheikh (an Iraqi government official), 'causing it to break down into different armed groups', and leading to 'a nationwide conflict that [by 2010 had] claimed the lives of over 100,000 Iraqis'.[38] Armed-group violence was a symptom of many things: the collapse of state authority, hatred of the US-led occupation and the unfreezing of ethno-religious interests that had been held in a repressive balance by Saddam Hussein.

The CPA was slow to respond to the brewing violence. US Department of Defense figures recorded the number of attacks in Iraq, from all causes, as quadrupling in the 12 months after June 2003. At this time, rather than monitoring the onset of insurgency, the CIA station in Baghdad was engaged in a fruitless search for weapons of mass destruction, Iraq's alleged development of which had been the main pretext for invasion.[39] The CPA drew criticism from Iraqis for having woefully inadequate plans to govern Iraq and for its failure to improve their living standards or restore security.[40] The CPA engaged in a 'de-Ba'athification' process, removing 30,000 former Ba'ath Party members from the public sector and dissolving the 400,000-strong Iraqi army.[41] As Iraq's state was dismantled, widespread looting took place and armed groups representing different sectors of Iraqi society filled the security vacuum. In late 2003 a memo from the CPA to Rumsfeld counted 30 armed groups, comprising some 30,000–60,000 'armed supporters'.[42]

In overall terms, right from the start, the United States' strategic aims were to reduce its military presence and leave a functioning, sovereign Iraqi government in its place. The Coalition was duly guided by the logic of choosing which armed groups to include and which to exclude from the state-building process. What followed was a series of selective judgements under CPA Order 92. According to Thomas Mowle, who served with the US military in Iraq in 2004:

> The CPA explicitly divided 'good' militias, those that had fought against Saddam, from 'bad' militias, those that appeared after the invasion. Groups that fought against Coalition forces were especially 'bad', were often considered terrorists, and so could not be negotiated with or rewarded.[43]

This led to a hastily organised transition scheme. The CPA treated Kurdish groups as the armed wings of an autonomous government-in-waiting in northern Iraq. For the leading Kurdish parties, the Kurdistan Democratic Party and Patriotic Union of Kurdistan, there was relief at the deposing of the Ba'athist regime. The Kurdish Peshmerga militia, numbering some 75,000, became the mandated security force of the autonomous Kurdistan Regional Government (KRG).

The Shia-dominated Badr Brigade was also legitimised. It was the armed wing of the Supreme Council for Islamic Revolution in Iraq (SCIRI), a political party opposed to Saddam's regime, and with long-standing ties to Iran.[44] The Badr Brigade joined the new Iraqi army, police and interior ministry in numbers, but their Iranian links and sectarian agenda would haunt security-sector reform.[45] SCIRI and another Shia party, Da'awa, 'could use their parts of the ministry to build up patronage networks and paramilitary and intelligence capabilities through official channels', observed Andrew Rathmell, a member of CPA staff and later an adviser on reform of Iraq's interior ministry.[46] Interior-ministry intelligence drew so heavily on the Badr Brigade that its religious practices were promoted in the ministry.

Iraq's security institutions were becoming sectarian fiefdoms, just as the CPA excluded other Shia groups from state institutions. Jaish al-Mahdi (JAM) was excluded because, as a grassroots movement that at the time lacked a recognised political party, the CPA considered that it lacked legitimacy.[47] JAM was also referred to as the Sadrists, named after their leader, influential Shia cleric Moqtada al-Sadr. The group was angry at being excluded from police and interior-ministry roles and instead carved out influence at street level.

The CPA also excluded those Sunnis who later waged an anti-occupation insurgency. The Sunni insurgency comprised several layers: former Ba'athists from Saddam's army and intelligence agencies; nationalists opposed to foreign occupation on patriotic grounds; and Sunni tribes previously allied to the Ba'athists. Some disenchanted Sunnis were open to the influence of Salafists, who were opposed to Western ideals being imposed on Iraq, and with whom al-Qaeda was aligned.[48]

Coalition efforts to restore order faltered during the CPA era. In the crucial 2003–04 period, to follow its policies through, the CPA needed to co-opt and coerce those armed groups that it had excluded from state structures.[49] This task was beyond its ability. A key moment came in April 2004, when Sunni insurgents in Fallujah, around 60 kilometres west of Baghdad, killed a group of US contractors. US forces attacked Fallujah to eliminate the city as a base for Sunni insurgents but ran into stiff resistance from a dug-in and well-armed defence. According to

Carter Malkasian, an academic and adviser to the US military in Iraq:

> The First Battle of Fallujah in April 2004 renders a cautionary lesson … The US launched the offensive into Fallujah in order to signal resolve and deter the population from supporting insurgent violence. Instead … [it] catalyzed popular support for insurgent violence in Iraq and threatened to turn the entire country against the Coalition.[50]

The Sunni insurgency entrenched itself in an area of central Iraq known as the 'Sunni triangle'. The US military was institutionally sluggish in comprehending the nature and extent of the insurgency. Nonetheless, the political process of handing power to the Iraqi state carried on. At the end of the CPA's tenure, in June 2004 it handed sovereignty to interim prime minister Ayad Allawi (2004–05). In 2005 Iraq held its first multi-party elections for 50 years, but they led to political deadlock and a transition government under Ibrahim al-Jaafari. It was not until the following year that Maliki was sworn in as prime minister, under the presidency of Jalal Talabani (2005–14), who held a more ceremonial role. Allawi and Maliki were Shia politicians, while Talabani was a Kurd. Sunni insurgents had little to gain from these new arrangements.

The war worsened in scale and increased in complexity. Former Ba'ath Party loyalists – overwhelmingly Sunnis – fought an anti-occupation war to retain their stake in post-Saddam Iraq. International jihadists of al-Qaeda in Iraq (AQI), led by Jordanian Abu Musab al-Zarqawi, entered the conflict to fight the US and offer Sunni insurgents a religious justification for their war. This unfolded contemporaneously with the Shia-majority population taking up arms to secure their own stake and fend off Sunni militants, notably doing so under Sadr. Iran, a Shia-majority state, backed the Sadrists.

Sectarian civil war beckoned. AQI escalated the violence with the suicide bombing of Shia targets. The 22 February 2006 bombing of the al-Askari mosque in Samarra, a sacred site to the Shia, was a touchstone moment. As Sunni and Shia death squads murdered each other's civilians, mainstream Iraqi leaders fanned the sectarian flames of Sunni–Shia intercommunal violence.[51]

The US surge: advancing along the military and political tracks (2007–2011)

The mood in Washington was bleak in the face of the Coalition's degenerating ability to influence Iraq's security. At this moment, Bush opted for a surge in the number of US troops. In 2007 he explained the strategy:

> The most urgent priority for success in Iraq is security, especially in Baghdad. Eighty per cent of Iraq's sectarian violence occurs within 30 miles of the capital … Our past efforts to secure Baghdad failed [because] there were not enough Iraqi and American troops to secure neighborhoods that had been cleared of terrorists and insurgents. And there were too many restrictions on the troops we did have.[52]

In late 2006, Bush had met Maliki to jointly endorse the fact that the US surge would target Shia as well as Sunni armed groups.[53] And it would also reflect a revised US doctrine. Petraeus, who had presided over the drafting of a COIN doctrine that sought to refocus how the US military fought insurgencies, took command of US forces in 2007 to oversee the application of this doctrine in Iraq. COIN emphasised relative restraint in the use of force, and making the security of the population, rather than the killing of militants, the barometer of success in undermining the armed groups.[54]

Consequently, during 2007–08, a change in US numbers and posture helped to break AQI and JAM.[55] US special forces engaged in targeted killings, weakening the Sunni insurgency, breaking AQI networks and killing Zarqawi.[56] The US also split apart the various layers of the Sunni insurgency. In what became known as the 'Anbar Awakening', Sunni tribes in Anbar province were peeled away from the insurgency. AQI had alienated these tribes by eroding their power base, and by the indiscriminate slaughter of its suicide bombings. Revulsion at AQI was a factor in the Sunni tribes' switching sides, but mainly they did so to avoid losing influence in Baghdad.[57] They could not overthrow Maliki's Shia-dominated government. Instead, by agreeing to cease their insurgency, Sunni tribal leaders were rewarded with political positions.[58] By working with the prevailing trends of Iraqi politics the conflict was dampened: the Shia were now the ruling majority, and it was for their leaders to dole out patronage to Sunnis as they saw fit.

The Shia rejectionist groups also had to be dealt with. Sadr declared a halt to attacks by JAM in August 2007, after pressure from US and newly trained Iraqi forces.[59] The security effort also played JAM against itself, empowering its Najaf-based core to purge its own more radical elements.[60] In Basra, in the south, where British forces had ceded control to JAM, Maliki presided over *Operation Charge of the Knights* in March 2008, to push out the armed groups. Maliki used newly raised Iraqi forces, with US airpower in support. This offensive was followed by further Iraqi operations against JAM in Baghdad's Sadr City.[61]

It was possible to deal selectively with parts of the insurgency at the time, precisely because it was so factionalised. In

Professor Ahmed Hashim's assessment, even at the height of the conflict, 'there was little if any coordination between Sunni and Shia insurgents'.[62] AQI, of course, remained the exception. Its nihilistic approach relied exclusively on violence to coerce the US and collapse Maliki's government. It was an irreconcilable element of the insurgency.

The surge – and Petraeus – gained a somewhat mythical status as having halted the catastrophic violence.[63] The problem was that by superimposing US military muscle on what was inherently an Iraqi situation, maintaining security could not be guaranteed. On 1 January 2009 the Coalition handed responsibility to Iraq for security of the fortified Green Zone in Baghdad, where government buildings were located. Coalition forces began to reduce their presence and withdrew fully in December 2011, after Iraq's government decided not to grant the US a Status of Forces Agreement (which would have been necessary to permit the continued basing of US forces in Iraq).[64] So draining had the conflict been for all involved, so costly in Iraqi lives, and so far adrift from the Coalition's envisaged outcomes, that Obama openly welcomed the fact that the US was done with military intervention in Iraq.

Epilogue: the Iraqi state inherits the challenge (2012–2014)
What followed is a cautionary tale in state-building through the selective legitimisation of armed groups. This approach, executed under the exigencies of a civil war, contributed to enshrining sectarianism in Iraqi politics. As Coalition forces gradually handed responsibility for security to the new Iraqi military – a process dubbed 'Iraqisation' – Iraq's new security forces took over from foreign soldiers, who reduced their role and left. A similar logic applied to the political track. As the Iraqi state became the main sovereign player, the Maliki government ultimately had to sanction political deals that the

Coalition only facilitated. The Iraqi state first supplemented, and then entirely replaced, the US as the main agent for engaging the remaining purveyors of non-state violence.

A new period of crisis brewed steadily. Instability began to return to Iraq by 2013, in part triggered by the civil war in adjacent Syria, but arising also from a crisis involving Maliki's government and Iraq's Sunnis. The Sunnis feared the dominant Shia would squeeze them out of key government and military positions. These fears of marginalisation appeared validated when, in December 2013, Maliki ordered the arrest of Sunni politician Ahmed al-Alwani. This galvanised Sunni protests against the government. Iraq's army had provoked this unrest through the heavy-handed nature of its arrest of Alwani and its suppression of the protesters. It led to a narrative of blame in the West – not without reason – that Maliki's sectarian slant had failed to hold together multi-ethnic Iraq.[65]

A storm broke in 2014 when an ISIS offensive routed the Iraqi army and captured huge tracts of Iraq. The group's declared aim was to establish a regional Islamic caliphate. The Maliki government was embattled, Baghdad vulnerable and the US humiliated that an armed Islamist group could fracture the sovereign Iraq that it had fought so hard to forge. The US launched airstrikes with other countries. To provide boots on the ground and assist Iraq's army, the US allied with Kurdish Peshmerga, while Iran backed Iraq's Shia militias. Iran, displaying its political clout with Baghdad's Shia politicians, also played a key role in forcing Maliki from power over his ineffectual response to ISIS. The new Iraqi prime minister, Haider al-Abadi, was named in August 2014.

In a decade-spanning conflict of such complexity, there are no clear lines of causality. It cannot be said that the US-led invasion, and the way that Iraq was patched back together, created the conditions under which ISIS could become a reality. Nor, for that matter, can it be said that Maliki's divisive leadership was the main factor of blame. Events in neighbouring Syria could not have been predicted and by 2014 the war was very much a regional affair. Nevertheless, the 2003 invasion had created enduring problems for Iraq, including Sunni marginalisation and heightened Kurdish aspirations for independence. Civil war in Syria and the rise of extremist Sunni groups fighting there only multiplied Iraq's problems. What has resulted is almost as far away from the outcomes envisaged in 2003 as one dares to imagine.

Engaging armed groups through partnerships

By coincidence, Karzai and Maliki ceased being presidents of their respective countries in 2014. By this point, exasperation was the governing sentiment in the state-building partnerships in Afghanistan and Iraq. The US was increasingly aghast at the character of the governments for which it had spilled blood, and at what it perceived as Karzai's tribal venality and Maliki's sectarianism. Conversely, Iraqis and Afghans were ambivalent towards the US for pursuing wars that seemed never to abate.

The state-building interventions of the post-9/11 era reflected a particular set of circumstances and, with hindsight, unrealistic US expectations. For all the resources and effort poured in from abroad, the gains following regime change have simply not been commensurate in either Afghanistan or Iraq. Nevertheless, the course of these conflicts illustrates themes that remain pertinent.

The first relates to the limitations of the COIN doctrine as a strategy. What COIN offered was a guide to using the US military to contain an insurgency. While it acknowledged the political roots of the violence, COIN doctrine needed to be coupled with local political processes and capacity to produce real strategic effect. Otherwise, foreign military muscle, which could not be sustained forever, would just hide the problem of weak local governments. No matter how long foreigners hold the reins of security and political measures, these will have to be handed over to the host state.

Both wars were waged as partnerships. But where does ownership of strategy sit when foreign governments support local governments? It lies neither entirely with the interveners nor with the locals, but somewhere in between. Progress amounts to the aggregated outcome of their efforts. In multilateral settings, such as NATO, the greater the share of the burden one takes, the greater say one is likely to have in deciding strategy. This axiom does not so readily apply to the burdens that are shared between foreign interveners and local partners. Neither party is naturally the 'senior' or 'bigger' partner. The fundamental imbalances – of an intervener with more resources, and of locals whose lands are at stake – do not balance out evenly. Instead, they can lead to strategic misdirection and poor outcomes. When multiple governments employ multiple policy approaches, armed groups can exploit the inevitable fissures, as can predatory regional powers.

The prospects for U-turns with armed groups are considerable. It should be remembered that in 2001, exploring a political deal with the Taliban seemed abhorrent to the US because of the death toll in the 9/11 attacks. In 2014, ISIS, understandably, was also deemed so abhorrent as to never merit anything other than an effort to fight and collapse the group. There is, of course, no parity between movements as distinct as the Taliban, al-Qaeda and ISIS. There is only a cautionary tale that in the desperate exigencies of collapsing states, and of wars that seemingly have no end, the notion of conflict giving way to some kind of begrudging compromise cannot be precluded. It is not impossible that over time the 'irreconcilable' may, in an altered form and in different circumstances, become 'reconcilable'.

Values and objectives play their parts in setting goals when engaging armed groups, but so do sheer levels of desperation. Strategy in such complex conflicts is always about relative gains. With so many overlapping local, regional and global interests at play, no actor – whether armed group, local government or foreign intervener – may achieve more than a fraction of what they set out to secure.

Notes

1 Hamid Karzai press conference, 16 November 2008, https://www.youtube.com/watch?v=ytI8ZyuSY2Y.

2 'Spiegel Interview with Iraqi Leader Nouri al-Maliki: "The Tenure of Coalition Troops in Iraq Should Be Limited"', *Der Spiegel*, 19 July 2008.

3 Vanda Felbab-Brown, *Aspiration and Ambivalence: Strategies and Realities of Counterinsurgency and State Building in Afghanistan* (Washington DC: Brookings Institution Press, 2013); Tim Bird and Alex Marshall, *Afghanistan: How the West Lost its Way* (New Haven, CT/London: Yale University Press, 2011); Seth Jones, *In the Graveyard of Empires: America's War in Afghanistan* (New York: W.W. Norton and Company, 2009).

4 The White House, 20 September 2001, http://georgewbush-whitehouse.archives.gov/infocus/bushrecord/documents/Selected_Speeches_George_W_Bush.pdf.

5 Ahmed Rashid, *Taliban* (London: Pan Macmillan, 2001).

6 James Dobbins, *After the Taliban: Nation-Building in Afghanistan* (Washington DC: Potomac Books, Inc., 2008), p. viii.

7 *Ibid.*, p. 72.

8 Felbab-Brown, *Aspiration and Ambivalence*, pp. 46–52, called these groups the three 'principal, comingled but distinct insurgency groups' in Afghanistan.

9 *Ibid.*, pp. 23–4; Rajiv Chandrasekaran, *Little America: The War Within the War for Afghanistan* (London: Bloomsbury Publishing, 2012), p. 86.

10 'Karzai Discusses Security, Pakistan with CODEL Dicks', 25 February 2007, released by Wikileaks.

11 Michael Semple, *Reconciliation in Afghanistan* (United States Institute for Peace, 2009); Chandrasekaran, *Little America*, p. 50.

12 Alex Strick van Linschoten and Felix Kuehn, *An Enemy We Created: The Myth of the Taliban Al-Qaeda Merger in Afghanistan, 1970–2010* (London: Hurst, 2012), pp. 245–54, 272–5; Bird and Marshall, *Afghanistan: How the West Lost its Way*, pp. 102, 113, 146, 155.

13 For sophisticated characterisations of the Taliban insurgency in Afghanistan see: Patrick Porter, *Military Orientalism: Eastern War Through Western Eyes* (London: Hurst, 2009), pp. 143–70; Strick van Linschoten and Kuehn, *An Enemy We Created*.

14 Bette Dam, *A Man and A Motorcycle: How Hamid Karzai Came to Power* (Utrecht: Ipso Facto Publishers, 2014).

15 'Scenesetter for December 10–11, 2008 visit to Afghanistan by SECDEF Robert M. Gates', 9 December 2008, released by Wikileaks.

16 Bob Woodward, *Obama's Wars: The Inside Story* (London: Simon & Schuster, 2010), p. 329; Chandrasekaran, *Little America*, p. 129.

17 Chandrasekaran, *Little America*, pp. 165–6.

18 *Ibid.*, p. 278.

19 Strick van Linschoten and Kuehn, *An Enemy We Created*, pp. 326–7.

20 Stephen Biddle, 'Ending the War in Afghanistan', *Foreign Policy*, September–October 2013, pp. 49–58. For consensus with this judgement, see: Woodward, *Obama's Wars*, pp. 346–8; Bird and Marshall, *Afghanistan: How the West Lost its Way*, pp. 259–60.

21 Karl Eikenberry, 'The Limits of Counterinsurgency Doctrine in Afghanistan', *Foreign Policy*, September–October 2013, pp. 59–74.

22 Vali Nasr, *The Dispensable Nation: American Foreign Policy in Retreat* (New York: Doubleday/Random House, 2013), pp. 25, 354; Biddle, 'Ending the War in Afghanistan', agrees that 'what the [US] has not done is spend the political capital needed for an actual deal', p. 50.

23 Chandrasekaran, *Little America*, pp. 223–4, 232, 234.

24 Quoted in *Ibid.*, p. 235.

25 Nasr, *The Dispensable Nation*, pp. 56–7.

26 Michael Hastings, 'The Runawat General', *Rolling Stone*, 8–22 July 2010, http://apj.us/pdf/rolling_stone-the_runaway_general.pdf.

27 Chandrasekaran, *Little America*, pp. 231, 300; Nasr, *The Dispensable Nation*, p. 42.

28 Nasr, *The Dispensable Nation*, p. 55.

29 Felbab-Brown, *Aspiration and Ambivalence*, pp. 233–41; Chandrasekaran, *Little America*, p. 290.

30 Patrick Porter, *Military Orientalism: Eastern War Through Western Eyes* (London: Hurst, 2009), p. 166.

31 Mark Urban, 'Duping of MI6 Reveals Afghan Coalition Flaws', BBC, 26 November 2010, http://www.bbc.co.uk/blogs/newsnight/markurban/2010/11/taliban_leaders_duping_of_mi6.html.

32 Jonathan Steele, 'Burhanuddin Rabbani: Obituary', *Guardian*, 21 September 2011, http://www.guardian.co.uk/world/2011/sep/21/burhanuddin-rabbani-obituary.

33 The White House, 1 May 2012, http://www.whitehouse.gov/the-press-office/2012/05/01/remarks-president-obama-address-nation-afghanistan.

34 Felbab-Brown, *Aspiration and Ambivalence*, pp. 30–1; Bird and Marshall, *Afghanistan: How the West Lost its Way*, pp. 228–9.

35 Strick van Linschoten and Kuehn, *An Enemy We Created*, p. 336.

36 Ashraf Ghani and Clare Lockhart, *Fixing Failed States: a Framework for Rebuilding a Fractured World* (Oxford: Oxford University Press, 2009), p. 12.

37 Felbab-Brown, *Aspiration and Ambivalence*, pp. 18, 22–3; Bird and Marshall, *Afghanistan: How the West Lost its Way*, pp. 250, 255.

38 Safa Rasul al-Sheikh and Emma Sky, 'Iraq since 2003: Perspectives on a Divided Society', *Survival: Global*

Politics and Strategy, vol. 53, no. 4, August–September 2011, p. 119, quoting casualty figures cited from http://www.irawbodycount.net.

[39] James Dobbins, Seth G. Jones and Benjamin Runkle, *Occupying Iraq: A History of the Coalition Provisional Authority* (Santa Monica, CA: RAND, 2009), pp. 94, 99.

[40] Tom Ricks, *Fiasco: the American Military Adventure in Iraq* (London: Allen Lane, 2006) documents planning failures within DoD; Rajiv Chandrasekaran, *Imperial Life in the Emerald City: Inside Iraq's Green Zone* (London: Bloomsbury Publishing, 2008) describes the impact of this negligent planning in the CPA; Dobbins et al., *Occupying Iraq* provides an account of Paul Bremer's team based on a survey of CPA memoranda; Rory Stewart, *Occupational Hazards: My Time Governing in Iraq* (London: Picador, 2007).

[41] Dobbins et al., *Occupying Iraq*, pp. 14–15, 28, 52–61, 104–5. The Iraqi Ministry of Defence and Intelligence Service were also disbanded, and looters pillaged and burned other ministry buildings.

[42] CPA memo from late 2003, quoted in *Ibid.*, p. 315.

[43] Thomas S. Mowle, 'Iraq's Militia Problem', *Survival: Global Politics and Strategy*, vol. 48, no. 3, 2006, p. 53.

[44] *Ibid.*, p. 46. SCIRI/Badr Brigade are Arab Shia, while Iran is predominantly Persian Shia.

[45] Toby Dodge, 'The US and Iraq', *Survival: Global Politics and Strategy*, vol. 52, no. 2, 2010, pp. 91–2; Andrew Rathmell, *Fixing Iraq's Internal Security Forces: Why is Reform of the*

Ministry of Interior so Hard?, Centre for Strategic and International Studies (November 2007), p. 7.

[46] Rathmell, *Fixing Iraq's Internal Security Force*, p. 7.

[47] Dobbins et al., *Occupying Iraq*, pp. 319–20; see also Mowle, 'Iraq's militia problem', p. 49 to explain JAM's exclusion.

[48] Ahmed Hashim, *Iraq's Sunni Insurgency*, Adelphi Paper 402 (London: IISS, 2008), pp. 17–25.

[49] Dobbins et al., *Occupying Iraq*, p. 312.

[50] Carter Malkasian, 'Signalling Resolve, Democratization, and the First Battle of Fallujah', *Journal of Strategic Studies*, vol. 29, no. 3, June 2006, pp. 423–52. See also: Dobbins et al., *Occupying Iraq*, pp. 311–12; Ricks, *Fiasco*, pp. 330–5.

[51] Yahia Said, 'Iraq in the Shadow of Civil War', *Survival: Global Politics and Strategy*, vol. 47, no. 4, 2005, pp. 85–92.

[52] George W. Bush, 'President's Address to the Nation', *New York Times*, 10 January 2007, http://www.nytimes.com/2007/01/11/us/11ptext.html?pagewanted=all.

[53] al-Sheikh and Sky, 'Iraq since 2003', p. 128.

[54] David Ucko, *The New Counterinsurgency Era: Transforming the US Military for Modern Wars* (Washington DC: Georgetown University Press, 2009).

[55] Dodge, 'The US and Iraq', p. 136.

[56] Thomas Ricks, *The Gamble: General Petraeus and the Untold Story of the American Surge in Iraq, 2006–2008* (London: Allen Lane, 2009).

[57] Austin Long, 'The Anbar Awakening', *Survival: Global Politics and Strategy*, vol. 50, no. 2, 2010, pp. 77–85, cites the example of Sheikh

Sattar al-Rishawi in Ramadi, who initiated his own resistance against AQI.

58 al-Sheikh and Sky, 'Iraq since 2003', pp. 124–7.

59 *Ibid.*, pp. 131–2.

60 Ricks, *The Gamble*, pp. 177, 242; al-Sheikh and Sky, 'Iraq since 2003', p. 134.

61 al-Sheikh and Sky, 'Iraq since 2003', p. 133

62 Hashim, *Iraq's Sunni Insurgency*, p. 73.

63 Ricks, *The Gamble*, pp. 24, 153, 259.

64 Dodge, 'The US and Iraq', p. 129; 'As Last US troops Leave Iraq, Obama and al-Maliki Chart Next Steps in Relationship', *Washington Post*, 12 December 2011.

65 'Going All Wrong: Civil Strife in Iraq', *The Economist*, 2 November 2013, pp. 52–3; Petraeus, 'Iraq Looks Worse Today Than it Did in 2006', 3 November 2013, http://www.twincities.com/2013/11/03/david-petraeus-iraq-looks-worse-today-than-it-did-in-2006/.

CHAPTER FIVE

The lopsided strategies of very weak or very strong states

> I never removed the goal of toppling Hamas … When I look around and see ISIS moving toward Jordan and already in Lebanon, with Hezbollah there already, supported by Iran, I defined the goal in the cabinet of delivering a hard blow to Hamas, and we did that.[1]
>
> Benjamin Netanyahu, 2014

> The ultimatum that we gave them has expired. We have said that at any moment the Congolese army with [the UN's] MONUSCO will start the operations against the FDLR armed group.[2]
>
> Joseph Kabila, 2015

To be credible, threats against armed groups need to be followed through, or else they are just empty words. If a state is especially weak relative to an armed group, or especially strong, this will influence how it weighs the options of force and accommodation. An especially weak state may have little choice but to cede ground to the armed groups it faces. Conversely, an especially strong state may see little worth in pursuing accommodation.

This chapter examines an example of strategy that has been forged in strength, and another of strategy forged in weakness.

Israel is a small, militarily powerful state that feels under little pressure to appease armed groups. Even if it cannot quite defeat Hamas, it can regularly punish it and refuse to yield to its pressure. Israel has duly concluded that it is in no hurry to forge a lasting peace with the Palestinians, stunting the political dimensions of its strategy, and infuriating foreign friends and foes alike. Israel's overreliance on its military abilities has even led it to be described as a contemporary Sparta.[3]

At the very opposite end of the spectrum, the Democratic Republic of the Congo (DRC) is a huge and conflict-ridden state saddled with a dysfunctional army. The modern DRC was forged through accommodations with armed groups after the Congolese wars of the 1990s. Instability has persisted since then, notably in the DRC's resistive eastern Kivu provinces bordering Rwanda. The DRC's army has been in no shape to take on armed groups there. As one report observed, it is 'the "military option" without an army'.[4]

It is truly a thing of wonder, perhaps even of absurdity, that sovereign statehood can encompass such diverse entities as Israel and the DRC. Aside from the shared badge of statehood they are unlike in almost every meaningful way. By juxtaposing these contrasting examples, this chapter examines lopsided strategies where one facet of a response has been persistently overemphasised. Lack of will or lack of capacity may leave states unwilling or unable to use multiple tracks. As past chapters have shown, it takes some governments a long time to break out of a single-track strategic mindset. But the reasons may well be structural, and rooted in the overwhelming weakness or strength of the state. Regardless, the outcome may be depressingly similar: confrontation, with no resolution in sight.

The DRC: a weak state forged from armed groups

It is not clear that statehood, in which central institutions and government are run from a capital, is an appropriate model for managing the vastness of the DRC, let alone bringing security to it. The tortured birth of the modern DRC state helps explain its weaknesses. Congo's implosion in the 1990s was catastrophic and complex. During this time, the armies of several intervening African governments, and numerous armed groups, fought in barely distinguishable ways. The current government in Kinshasa has its roots in a rebel group. Its sovereignty was established by a political transition in the 2000s, with President Joseph Kabila elected to office in 2006. This case study primarily focuses on this period, albeit by providing the context to understand why the Kinshasa government has had little actual presence in so many areas it nominally governs across the DRC's landlocked expanse.

To create the modern DRC state, the remnants of several armed groups were brought into the national army, the Armed Forces of the DRC (FARDC). The international community funded disarmament, demobilisation and reintegration (DDR) of ex-combatants, and security-sector reform (SSR), to help the DRC emerge from its wars and build a durable state. Instead, for Kinshasa's government, DDR and SSR have become lifelines that enable the regime to survive and dismantle its rivals.[5] First run by president Laurent Kabila (1997–2001), the DRC has since been run by his son. The picture that emerges is of an embattled state, run by a single family, opportunistically cutting deals with warlords by bringing them into the national military.[6] The FARDC's weaknesses left it dependent on UN peacekeepers to fight in the Kivu provinces – which the UN Organization Stabilization Mission in the Democratic Republic of the Congo (MONUSCO) only began to do robustly in 2013. Ultimately, the DRC has lacked a security apparatus with which to impose its will on armed groups, tilting its default approach towards accommodation and reliance on the UN.

The First and Second Congo Wars and the birth of the DRC (1996–2002)

No single line of reasoning explains why war came to the DRC, why it expanded to the magnitude it did, and why conflict persisted in the eastern DRC. For author Jason Stearns:

> Like layers of an onion, the Congo war contains wars within wars. There was not one Congo war, or even two, but at least forty or fifty different, interlocking wars. Local conflicts fed into regional and international conflicts and vice-versa.[7]

The scale of devastation was enormous. Millions died, mostly from displacement and disease that resulted from the wars. It is a conflict that eludes easy categorisation, given the closely interwoven themes of state failure, ethnic violence, resource looting and outside meddling. The sheer number of warlords, rebellions and militias littering recent Congolese history are bewildering. To make sense of them here, it is useful to consider the DRC through the prism of an acutely weak state. Its institutions and army have struggled to stop myriad local grievances from being expressed in violent fashion. And it has been unable to stop predatory African states from exploiting these grievances by waging proxy wars in the DRC to extract its resources for their own profit.

The reasons for Congolese state weakness are geographic, demographic and historic. A multi-ethnic state covering a huge territory, its borders are a product of the 'Scramble for Africa'. Belgian colonial rule began in 1908. After independence in 1960, a UN intervention was required to stop the southeastern Katanga region from seceding.[8] Economically, politically and socially underdeveloped under Belgian rule, Congo then suffered under the dictatorship of Mobutu Sese Seko, who ruled from 1965 until 1997 and renamed the country Zaire.

War came from over the border as a result of conflict in Rwanda in 1994. The Belgian colonial practice of moving Tutsis to Congo's fertile Kivu provinces for plantation work, from present-day Rwanda, linked Congo to this ethnic fault line. The *Banyarwanda* (people who came from Rwanda) competed with the other eastern Congolese peoples, notably the Hutu communities of the Kivu region, for resources. These cross-border ethnic links were fuel to be ignited by Rwanda's implosion into war and genocide, as Hutus slaughtered Tutsis.

By July 1994, a resurgent Tutsi force, the Rwandan Patriotic Front (RPF), led by future Rwandan president Paul Kagame, had defeated the Hutu génocidaires. From its base in Uganda, Kagame's RPF advanced into Rwanda, drove the Hutu forces into eastern Congo and pursued them there. Out of this action, one of the most surprising themes of Congo's wars emerged. Rwanda, a fraction of the size of its neighbour, proceeded to use the pretext of hunting génocidaires to try to turn eastern Congo into a virtual dependency.[9]

Rwanda's genocide did not cause the First Congo War (1996–97), but it was the catalyst.[10] The root cause was Mobutu's weakening rule, domestically and regionally. Rwanda and Uganda conspired to oust Mobutu. They picked Laurent Kabila to run the Alliance of Democratic Forces for the Liberation of Congo (ADFL), an armed group they created. To defend his regime, Mobutu armed Hutu refugees in eastern Congo. This did not stop the ADFL, which was backed by regional powers all seeking to overthrow Mobutu after his three decades in power – and in doing so, to gain a slice of Congolese wealth.

In 1997 the ADFL captured Kinshasa. Laurent Kabila pronounced himself president. Zaire was renamed the DRC. Once in power, Kabila tried to break free from his Ugandan and Rwandan patrons, triggering the Second Congo War (1998–2003). Rwanda and Uganda now tried to remove Kabila by creating a new Tutsi armed group, the Rally for Congolese Democracy (RCD). This time, they did not achieve regime change, as Kabila countered by securing other alliances. Angola and Zimbabwe backed him and, in a volte-face, Kabila armed his former Hutu foes to fight the invading Tutsi RCD. These Congolese Hutu armed groups became known as the Mai-Mai.[11]

The war involved a third group. Jean-Pierre Bemba's Movement for the Liberation of Congo (MLC) started its own rebellion in northern DRC. The MLC was backed by Uganda, and by former Mobutu supporters (Bemba had been a Mobutu protégé).[12] Then, disagreement between Uganda and Rwanda over how to fight their war against Kabila boiled over. Uganda felt sidelined by the extent to which Rwanda was dictating the war, and their own respective proxies began fighting each other, compounding the chaos.[13]

The outcome of this many-sided war was stalemate. Exhaustion led several key state and non-state combatants to the negotiating table.[14] Regional powers signed the Lusaka Accord in July 1999, but it did not last. In January 2000 it was announced that a UN Mission (MONUC) would deploy to the DRC, under a UN Chapter VII mandate for peace enforcement. However, Laurent Kabila was determined to keep fighting. To maximise his battlefield gains he launched new offensives and tried to delay the deployment of MONUC.[15]

Laurent Kabila's assassination by a bodyguard in January 2001 helped to end the Second Congo War. His son Joseph took over and at the Sun City Agreement in April 2002 agreed to a

ceasefire with the RCD and MLC. So too did many of the intervening regional powers, keen to cut their losses. Angola and
Zimbabwe concluded that they had saved Kabila from being
overthrown. Uganda, weary of its clashes with Rwanda, also
quit the war. Ending Rwandan interference would be tougher.
In October 2002 US president George W. Bush and South
African president Thabo Mbeki convened talks with Joseph
Kabila and Kagame, who promised that Rwanda-backed forces
would leave the DRC.[16] Holding Kagame to this promise has
troubled the international community ever since.

The state that shakily emerged from the Second Congo War
was a product of battlefield realities. While Joseph Kabila's
forces controlled areas around the capital, the MLC held the
north and the RCD the south. A state was cobbled together, but
other combatants were left at large. Mai Mai and Interahamwe
– former Hutu génocidaires – were not present at Sun City.
Nevertheless, in December 2002 a deal was signed in Pretoria.
Joseph Kabila would remain president and, in a power-sharing
deal known as '1+4', he would have four vice-presidents, one of
each from the government, the RCD, the MLC and civil society.
Joseph Kabila, himself a product of the ADFL rebellion, would
share power with other former rebels.

Why the DRC accommodated or ceded ground to armed groups (2003–2011)

This transitional government formally took charge in 2003,
until national elections in 2006 saw Kabila defeat Bemba of
the MLC. The RCD had also become a political party, but its
enduring associations with Rwanda led it to do badly at the
polls. This political transition was closely connected to establishing security. And security hinged on demobilising armed
groups and building a nationally representative army. In this,
the fledgling DRC state faced an uphill struggle.

Legal scholar Filip Reyntjens explains the new government's weak position:

> Although there was no state worth mentioning and a whole half the national territory was outside government control, Kabila represented a sovereign legal entity recognized by the international community. This recognition of juridical, rather than empirical statehood, gave him an edge over his challengers, and it allowed him to get away with an erratic mode of governance … It allowed Kabila to 'play state'.[17]

The situation was not uniform across the DRC. In some parts of the country various armies (Congolese, Rwandese, Zimbabwean and Angolan) and their militias had, as academic and historian Gérard Prunier writes, 'fought semi-professionally and could therefore be physically stopped and evacuated elsewhere'. But in the eastern DRC, the crucible of the conflict, 'bringing under control the myriad feuding units was akin to trying to harness a bunch of wild horses to a cart'.[18]

The policy response, backed by the international community, was to co-opt former rebels into a new national army, the FARDC.[19] During the war, Zimbabwean and Angolan contingents, Rwandan Hutus and Burundian mercenaries had all supplemented Kabila's army. During the 2003–06 transition, the Congolese core of Kabila's force integrated with the RCD and MLC.[20] But the FARDC could do little when faced with the resumption of insurgency in the eastern DRC.

Part of the problem was mindset and proximity. A vast distance separates Kinshasa and the eastern provinces of North and South Kivu, which border Rwanda, and Ituri, bordering Uganda. Kinshasa's political elite did not intuitively perceive these provinces as core to their interests, leaving them open to persistent Rwandan meddling. Without UN assistance, it is unlikely that the DRC would have been able to prevent losing control of them completely.[21]

This threat almost became real in 2004, as General Laurent Nkunda began an insurgency against the DRC. Nkunda had refused to join the FARDC. A former RCD commander, and a Tutsi from North Kivu, he claimed to be protecting Tutsis from Hutu génocidaires. In reality, Nkunda was a Rwandan proxy.[22] Kabila ordered a military offensive against Nkunda, but the FARDC could not stop him. Nkunda, who formed the National Congress for the Defence of the People (CNDP) as the vehicle for his insurgency, also fought UN peacekeepers in a drive to capture Goma, the main city in the Kivu provinces. Senior DRC military officials negotiated with Nkunda, asking him to cease his insurgency and join the FARDC. Nkunda eventually agreed, but turned this to his advantage, using his co-option into the FARDC to expand the number of forces personally loyal to him.

Why had creating a paid, disciplined and nationally representative army proved so hard? The Congolese security sector had historically weak foundations. Belgian colonists had purposefully kept the army weak, and Congolese were prevented from advancing beyond the rank of sergeant. Under Mobutu, the army was again kept weak to reduce the prospects of a coup, as Mobutu invested in personally loyal paramilitaries.[23] In line with this practice, Joseph Kabila would build a strong presidential guard, while much of the FARDC remained poorly paid. Prunier summarises the consequences:

> The FARDC were set up to fuse the various armed groups into one national army. But the various warlords tended to keep some troops outside FARDC as a military insurance policy … *mixage* (when troops of various ethnic origins serve in the same units) and

brassage (when troops are stationed in parts of the country away from their ethnic homeland) are still far from completed, in the east particularly, and many units of the FARDC are 'national' in name only.[24]

This has not been welcome news for international funders of DDR and SSR in the DRC. The international community has supported efforts to build a durable state and representative national army. But Kabila's priority has been to buy off rivals by nominally inducting them into the national army. The size-able disconnect between the aspirations of the international community and those of the regime in Kinshasa would never truly be addressed.[25]

The DDR and SSR processes ran concurrently as ex-combatants were used to stand up new security forces. Some demobilised fighters returned to village life while others (often those already possessing a firearm) were fast-tracked into the FARDC. By the time DDR came to an official end in September 2011, around 20,000 demobilised combatants had been integrated into the security forces.[26] In the context of the wars from which the DRC had emerged, this was an achievement. In creating a competent FARDC, the process was plagued with problems, including recidivism and indiscipline. A leader might be integrated into the FARDC but his fighters desert him to join another armed group.[27] Some demobilised fighters joined the FARDC only to pursue their own goals, such as looting or defending their own kin. Roger Meece, then head of the UN mission (renamed from MONUC to MONUSCO in 2010), said of the process: 'What you're doing is integrating members of an armed gang into the army.'[28]

The weakness of its army left the DRC with no workable military options. Accommodation was the only option to deal with Nkunda's rebellion. In January 2008 the Goma Agreement was reached between the DRC government, Nkunda's CNDP and Mai Mai groups – but Rwanda was not involved. On 23 March 2009 another agreement was signed, this time between the DRC and Rwandan governments. It stipulated that the CNDP would be broken up and its remnants integrated into the FARDC, and that Rwanda would arrest Nkunda, which it did in 2009. In return, as an offering to Rwanda, the FARDC, backed by the UN, would mount offensives against armed Hutu group the Democratic Forces for the Liberation of Rwanda (FDLR).

In the resulting *Operation Amani Leo* in 2010, the FARDC took on the FDLR.[29] As it did so, however, the brazen manner in which the FARDC profited and pillaged during its advance meant that it only contributed to the chaos in the eastern DRC. Meece was clear: 'the leading cause of insecurity is a collection of foreign and domestic armed groups in the east. The FARDC problem is that it is inadequate to be able to respond.'[30] The sovereign authority of the DRC was still fictional in the east. The end of Nkunda's uprising only interrupted the violence.

Against the M23 rebellion – the UN adds a military option (2012–2014)

In April 2012, Bosco Ntaganda began a new insurgency. Nicknamed 'the terminator', he was a military commander in Nkunda's CNDP, and led a breakaway faction that mutinied and left the FARDC. Ntaganda complained that the DRC had reneged on the terms of the 23 March 2009 deal (from which his M23 group derived its name). Once again, Rwanda played a role, backing M23, which was a Tutsi group, in its bid to capture Goma, which it did in 2012, defeating the FARDC. History was repeating itself.

This time the UN responded muscularly. A MONUSCO 'Intervention Brigade' was mandated according to UN Resolution 2098:

> To carry out targeted offensive operations … to prevent
> the expansion of all armed groups, neutralize these
> groups, and to disarm them in order to contribute to the
> objective of reducing the threat posed by armed groups
> on state authority and civilian security in eastern DRC
> and to make space for stabilization activities.[31]

The UN Intervention Brigade comprised around 3,000 personnel from Tanzania, Malawi and South Africa, organised in two infantry battalions. By late 2013, with nominal FARDC support, the UN force had inflicted a defeat on M23, assisted by its helicopters and drones. Martin Kobler, who became the head of MONUSCO in 2013, confidently declared that 'the era of cohabitation between armed groups and the UN is over'.[32]

The UN/FARDC offensive occurred in parallel with negotiations in Kampala involving M23. These talks provoked a split in the group. As his battlefield position slipped, Ntaganda was willing to sign a peace deal, but others in the group were not. This left M23 in disarray. In January 2014, Joseph Kabila announced an amnesty for surrendering M23 rebels, while Rwanda came under international pressure to end its support for M23. In March 2014 Ntaganda decided that he could not rely on Rwandan protection and sought refuge at the US embassy in Kigali. The exact pressures leading to Ntaganda's decision are unclear, but the defeat of the M23 movement was a direct precursor to this outcome, and to Ntaganda's later trial at the International Criminal Court.

The decisive defeat of M23 was a rare success involving the combined use of coercive force, negotiations with the rebels and regional diplomacy. In many ways, it is the exception that proves a rule of concessions to armed groups that has largely held since the DRC state emerged in the 2000s. Is this success replicable? The Hutu FDLR and the Mai Mai groups present further challenges in the eastern DRC. And instability is not confined to the eastern DRC, with the resource-rich southern Katanga province experiencing secessionist violence in 2013.

The DRC has seen armed groups repeatedly appear and take advantage of the proliferation of arms, the security vacuum, and the persistence of ethnic and regional grievances. In response, Kinshasa has tended to manage its security woes with short-term concerns in mind, and by ceding ground to, or nominally accommodating, its rivals.[33] The FARDC has at times wrought as much havoc as the armed groups it has faced. Even with selective and robust UN interventions, it is difficult to envisage how the DRC can durably contain the endemic armed-group violence that it faces. Such is the fate of a chronically weak state.

Israel's perpetual security dilemma in the Palestinian territories

Israel's discernibly lopsided policy mix, with security considerations given undue prominence, reflects its history of being besieged by enemies. A Jewish state in a Muslim region, Israel was born into insecurity. Formerly, the main threat came from Arab states it fought in the wars of 1948, 1967, 1973 and 1982. Over time, as the Arab states met repeated defeat, they saw greater gain in avoiding war with Israel, despite the unresolved nature of their fundamental disagreements. This balance has largely held until today, even in the face of continuing regional stresses. In the twenty-first century, Israel has perceived threats from Iran's efforts to build nuclear weapons, from Syria's collapse into civil war, and from political instability and regime changes in Egypt. But Israel has drawn the lesson that its military strength – and its undeclared nuclear arsenal – have deterred its regional rivals.[34]

The most acute, direct, day-to-day security threats Israel faces are from armed groups. The era of Arab–Israeli wars is long since over. The Israel Defense Forces (IDF) has reoriented its capabilities accordingly.[35] Israel has not, however, similarly reoriented its political strategies to managing the armed-group threats. Its default response has been a militarised one. Chief among the armed-group threats to Israel is Hamas.

The politics of resistance is at the core of Hamas. Rooted in the Palestinian territories, it has waged a resistance war against the Israeli occupation of Gaza. Hamas represents the militarisation of Palestinian discontent towards Israel, acting as a spoiler in past peace processes. In 2006 Hamas became the elected governing authority in the Gaza Strip. This has brought its relations with Israel into a new stage, far removed from its origins in 1987 as a street-level protest movement. Thus, despite its use of terrorism, Hamas also developed as a political movement with leverage over the Palestinian territories. This leverage has only grown since Israel's military withdrawal from Gaza in 2005.[36]

How is it, then, that Israel's response has remained defined by its security operations? Israel appears trapped in cyclical confrontations, mounting periodic military offensives, but never bringing encounters to anything approaching a discernible outcome. Arguably, the Israeli state is unable to articulate what such an outcome might entail. According to Professor Daniel Byman:

> Many of Israel's problems come down to the issue of tactics versus strategy. The Israelis are unusually strong tactically ... At the same time, Israel often blunders from crisis to crisis without a long-term plan for how to solve the problem once and for all. The day-to-day maintenance of counterterrorism often does not

reflect, and at times is even in opposition to, broader goals, such as stable peace with the Palestinians, or Israel's diplomatic interests.[37]

Israeli political and military leaders, not only outside observers, have tended to assume that their security problems can never be solved, only managed.[38] Avraham Shalom, who led the Israeli domestic-intelligence agency, Shin Bet, between 1981 and 1986, shares this view, complaining that 'there was no strategy, just tactics'.[39]

Israel's stability in decades to come may well be better guaranteed by a more balanced response to the socio-economic and demographic challenges presented by the Palestinian territories. Achieving this, while still guaranteeing Israel's security, is a policy challenge demanding multiple tracks. In practice, Israel's response remains defined by the single track of its security policies.

As Israel talks to Arafat's Fatah, Hamas emerges as its rival (1987–1999)

Israel has played the politics of peace by talking to the Palestinian Authority (PA), which is run by Fatah, a group founded in 1959, but has been loath to talk to Hamas. This is because Hamas emerged as an alternative to the core Palestinian national movement. In other words, as the Palestinian national cause has bifurcated between Hamas and Fatah, Israel's strategic response has become similarly bifurcated: security measures against Hamas, and dialogue with the PA.

Well before Hamas existed, Israel was already experienced in fighting Palestinian militants. Fatah built its early reputation on militancy and came to dominate the Palestine Liberation Organization (PLO), which was recognised in 1964 by Arab states as the Palestinian's representative body. The 1967 war, and the start of Israeli occupation of Palestinian areas, was Fatah's opportunity to come to prominence, by raiding Israel from sanctuaries in Syria and Jordan. In 1969, Fatah's leader Yassir Arafat became PLO chairman. The PLO proceeded to lead the Palestinian cause from abroad, but kept having to move its base. Jordanian authorities evicted the PLO in 1970, and so it moved to Lebanon, where it stayed until Israel invaded that country in 1982, prompting its move to Tunisia. This itinerant existence allowed the PLO to survive, but left it disengaged from the changing popular currents of Palestinian opinion.[40]

This is the space that Hamas would fill, emerging as an alternative at a critical moment in the Palestinian cause. The First Intifada, a street-level Palestinian uprising against Israeli occupation, began in December 1987. Hamas, which means 'Islamic Resistance Movement', formed that year. Co-founder Sheikh Yassin drew on the popular struggle in Gaza and the West Bank, where Palestinian youths resisted Israeli security forces. Yassin keenly distinguished Hamas from Arafat's PLO, which by now was rejecting militancy and embracing negotiation. Arafat's approach initially paid dividends, as Israel accepted the PLO as a negotiating partner, and held talks under Norwegian auspices. On the White House lawn, under the gaze of US president Bill Clinton, Arafat and Israeli prime minister Yitzhak Rabin signed the Oslo Accord peace deal in September 1993.

During the Oslo peace process Israel managed a multi-track policy response. But it was attempting to pursue politics separately from its counter-terrorism objectives. So great was Rabin's desire for a deal with the PLO that he came to tolerate a level of violence by Palestinian spoilers that proved politically and personally fatal. Ami Ayalon, Shin Bet director between 1995 and 2000, has characterised Israeli strategy during the Oslo process in this way: 'We will fight terror as if there is no peace process, and continue the peace process as if there is no terror.'[41]

This terror was being perpetrated by Hamas and an older group, Palestinian Islamic Jihad (PIJ). Their suicide bombings were reaping a deadly toll in Israeli cities, which placed Rabin in an invidious position. Israeli hardliners accused him of selling them out, and of making concessions to one set of Palestinians while another set persisted with terrorism. One of these hardliners assassinated Rabin in November 1995. The Oslo process suffered a huge blow, but attempts were made to ensure its continuation.

This meant Arafat could still claim progress in the Palestinian cause through the peace process. The Oslo Accord legitimised the PLO through the creation of the PA. The PA had limited governance over Gaza and the West Bank, albeit without statehood. After Oslo, however, the PA – and hence Fatah – would increasingly be defined by its dysfunctional, corrupt administration.[42] Had Oslo been fully implemented, Hamas would have been dismantled. Instead, it was now at the vanguard of Palestinian resistance and continued to violently oppose Israel, its goal to reclaim Palestine with Jerusalem as its capital.[43]

Israel resorts to counter-terrorism as the peace process withers (2000–2005)

The strands of Israel's response became more disconnected during the Second Intifada. It started in September 2000 after Ariel Sharon, then a prime-ministerial candidate, provoked popular Palestinian anger by visiting the Temple Mount, a religious site in Jerusalem sacred to Jews and Muslims. Hamas's military wing, the Qassam brigade, responded with a suicide-bombing campaign. In 2002 alone, Israel suffered 53 suicide attacks by Hamas and smaller groups such as PIJ and the al-Aqsa Martyrs' Brigade. Shin Bet faced the daunting task of countering these attacks, given the short distances suicide bombers needed to travel from the Palestinian territories to Israeli cities. The IDF responded with *Operation Defensive Shield* in March–May 2002. It blockaded Arafat's PA compound in Ramallah, in the West Bank, but in Gaza, where Hamas was carving out a power base, the IDF found it far harder to exert control.[44]

International opprobrium was heaped on Israel for its apparent collective punishment of the Palestinians. Amid the descent into violence there were efforts to control the fighting. At several points in 2001–03 Hamas opted for short truces to allow dialogue. The reciprocal violence of suicide bombs and IDF operations would interrupt every truce. Influential figures on both sides advocated not only a ceasefire, but that Hamas should join the political process. They included Efraim Halevy, director of Israel's foreign-intelligence agency, Mossad, between 1998 and 2002, and Abu Shanab, a moderate Hamas leader who argued in favour of stopping suicide attacks. Theirs were not the dominant voices, however. Hardline opinion won out on both sides. Hamas remained a spoiler group and Israel tilted ever further towards relying on security measures – and increasingly on targeted killings.[45]

Abu Shanab was killed in an Israeli airstrike in August 2003. Wheelchair-bound Hamas leader Sheikh Yassin was killed in March 2004 and the following month his successor Abdel Aziz al-Rantissi was also killed. By decapitating the Hamas leadership, the IDF hoped to maximise pressure on the group. However, it could not bring Hamas to collapse.

By early 2005 both sides were moving towards an agreement to halt the Second Intifada. Hamas agreed to a ceasefire, which allowed the PA to come to an agreement with Sharon, now prime minister, in February 2005. In August the IDF withdrew from Gaza – a policy change pushed for by Sharon in the face of bitter opposition from the Israeli settler community. It marked the end of 38 years of an Israeli military presence in the Gaza Strip following the 1967 war. What impact would this have on Israel's relations with Hamas?

Israel's policy towards Hamas after withdrawing from Gaza (2006–2014)

Security-wise, the withdrawal from Gaza was a change to Israel's approach. For Sharon, the Hamas challenge should be dealt with at arm's length, relying on a security barrier Israel was building around the Palestinian territories, on Israel's intelligence coverage and its ability to respond with airstrikes and raids to future transgressions by Hamas. The change in tack was to leave Gaza even more open for Hamas to consolidate its local standing.

Hamas was politically ascendant. Its defiance of Israel continued with occasional suicide bombs and it now also openly challenged Fatah. The death of Arafat in November 2004 had marked a generational change in the Palestinian national cause. Mahmoud Abbas, also a Fatah member, now ran the PA. Hamas chose not to recognise Abbas and the PA. This choice was vindicated when, in January 2006, Hamas defeated Fatah in the Palestinian legislative elections. So emboldened was Hamas that it mounted a military overthrow of Fatah in Gaza in 2007. Fighting between the Palestinian factions ensued. Fatah's authority in the PA was increasingly restricted to the West Bank. Hamas was allowed to run Gaza, leaving Israel to wrestle with the problem of dealing with an armed group that Gaza residents had popularly elected.[46]

Since Hamas took political power in Gaza, there has been little maturation in relations with the Israeli state. Notably, in 2007 the al-Aqsa Martyrs' Brigade took up an amnesty programme backed by Shin Bet, in exchange for positions in the official security forces of the PA. Hamas, however, decided to remain apart. A bitter retaliatory cycle has ensued, in which periodic IDF military operations are launched in response to Hamas terrorist and rocket attacks.

In June 2006 Hamas kidnapped an IDF soldier, Gilad Shalit. Israel responded with an economic blockade and strikes on Gaza. It later escalated with *Operation Cast Lead* (December 2008–January 2009), as the IDF attacked Gaza in a three-week incursion, killing many Palestinians and demolishing homes. Israel wanted to make Hamas pay a high price for its violence.[47] The deterrent effect did not last, however. *Operation Pillar of Defence* (November 2012) was an eight-day IDF operation mounted in response to the Qassam brigade firing rockets from Gaza into Israeli cities. During the operation the IDF killed Hamas intelligence chief Ahmed Jabari in a drone strike on his car.

Such tactical successes have not produced lasting answers to the strategic conundrum of how to engage Hamas, and with what end in mind. Back channels between Israel and Hamas exist. American Israeli Gershon Baskin helped negotiate Shalit's release in 2011 by talking separately to the office of Prime Minister Benjamin Netanyahu, and then to Hamas leader Khaled Mashal and Ismail Haniyeh of Hamas's political wing, passing messages between the sides. Both sides denied that the channel existed.[48] These denials are understandable. As long as Hamas refuses to accept Israel's legitimacy, it is hard to imagine how Israel would countenance overt talks.

Yet the choices open to Israel may well narrow. In 2013 the US renewed its diplomatic drive to restart the peace process, in the wake of the Palestinian territories gaining UN observer status in November 2012 – an accomplishment for Abbas and the PA. The path to Palestinian statehood, if it were to gather momentum, would force Israel to reconsider how to engage

Hamas as part of a wider engagement with the Palestinians. Otherwise, Hamas would retain its ability to spoil the process. The prospects seemed negligible, however, after the IDF launched *Operation Protective Edge* into Gaza in July 2014 – yet another crackdown against Hamas, ostensibly to stop rocket attacks, and after Hamas members killed three Israeli teenagers in the West Bank.

Wearily, the world watches the retaliatory cycle of rocket fire, terrorism and Israeli operations. Behind the scenes, Israel's security community dominates policymaking. Despite the military resumés of most senior Israeli leaders, their focus has been tactical and operational, not strategic. As Byman observes, 'often Israel's top officials thought only about what to do next rather than what they wanted in the end'.[49] In Shalom's judgement:

> All in all, we gained control over the war on terror. We kept it on a low flame so the country could do what it wanted. That's important, but it didn't solve the problem of occupation. What it did was, instead of 20 attacks a week, there were 20 a year.[50]

The instinct for revenge, in the face of bitter terrorist blows, has been a feature of Israeli policy. In the words of Ayalon: 'How many operations did we launch because we hurt, because when they blow up buses it really hurts us and we want revenge?'[51]

In a hypothetical policy mix, in which Israel used counter-terrorism in the service of its negotiations, such a strategic shift would demand painful compromises. It may be less saleable to the Israeli people, who understandably prefer to be protected from, rather than bullied by, terrorists. A policy mix that placed a revived peace process at its core would require restraint from Israeli security forces, who would have to refrain from killing militants, even if they acquired actionable intelligence. Even then, the negotiations may go nowhere, and may falter over such perennial disputes as future borders, the status of Palestinian refugees and control of Jerusalem.[52]

Taking stock of its policy towards Hamas, however, Israel's strategy seems lopsided, trapped by the inertia of security measures that lack accompanying political approaches. Zeev Maoz concludes that 'Israel will need to be as bold in its diplomacy as it has been in its use of force'.[53] Israel's strategic challenge resides in achieving its security aims, while addressing the needs of long-term peace with the Palestinians and regional relations in the Middle East. How Israel engages Hamas is a crucial component of these challenges. An Israel that takes any steps towards reconciling with Hamas is hard to envisage, but some Israeli securocrats realise their dilemma. As Shin Bet director Avi Dichter (2000–05) said: 'You can't make peace using military means. Peace must be built on a system of trust, after, or without using military means.'[54]

Notes

1 'Netanyahu: Toppling Hamas Remains an Option', *Jerusalem Post*, 30 August 2014, http://www.jpost.com/Israel-News/Politics-And-Diplomacy/Netanyahu-Toppling-Hamas-remains-an-option-372828.

2 'UN and DRC Forces Prepare For War', Al-Jazeera, 16 January 2015, http://america.aljazeera.com/articles/2015/1/16/congo-hutu-war.html.

3 Zeev Maoz, *Defending the Holy Land: A Critical Analysis of Israel's Security and Foreign Policy* (Ann Arbor: University of Michigan Press, 2006), p. 6.

4 International Crisis Group, 'Eastern Congo: Why Stabilisation Failed' (Africa Briefing 91, 4 October 2012), p. 11.

5 'Small Arms Survey,' 'Demobilization in the DRC: Armed Groups and the Role of Organizational Control', Armed Actors Issue Brief Number 1 (Geneva: Small Arms Survey, April 2013), p. 1.

6 Interviews with Guillaume Lacaille, former political adviser to MONUSCO, and Nico Tillon, DRC programme officer at Conciliation Resources, October 2013.

7 Jason Stearns, *Dancing in the Glory of Monsters: The Collapse of the Congo and the Great War of Africa* (New York: Public Affairs, 2012), p. 69.

8   James Dobbins et al., *The UN's Role in Nation Building: From Congo to Iraq* (Santa Monica, CA: RAND, 2005), pp. 5–23.

9   Gerard Prunier, *From Genocide to Continental War: The Congolese Conflict and the Crisis of Contemporary Africa* (London: Hurst & Company, 2009), p. 285.

10   Prunier, *From Genocide to Continental War*, p. xxxi.

11   Stearns, *Dancing in the Glory of Monsters*, pp. 250–1.

12   *Ibid.*, pp. 223–5.

13   Prunier, *From Genocide to Continental War*, p. 220.

14   Filip Reyntjens, *The Great African War: Congo and Regional Geopolitics, 1996–2006* (Cambridge: Cambridge University Press, 2009), p. 8.

15   Stearns, *Dancing in the Glory of Monsters*, pp. 271, 284; Séverine Autesserre, *The Trouble with the Congo: Local Violence and the Failure of International Peacebuilding* (Cambridge: Cambridge University Press, 2010), p. 48.

16   Prunier, *From Genocide to Continental War*, pp. 265–6, 272, 285.

17   Reyntjens, *The Great African War*, p. 232.

18   Prunier, *From Genocide to Continental War*, p. 337.

19   Small Arms Survey, 'Demobilization in the DRC: Armed Groups and the Role of Organizational Control'.

20   International Crisis Group, 'Eastern Congo: Why Stabilisation Failed' (Africa Briefing 91, 4 October 2012), p. 2; Reyntjens, *The Great African War*, p. 262.

21   Reyntjens, *The Great African War*, p. 207; Prunier, *From Genocide to Continental War*, p. 281.

22   Stearns, *Dancing in the Glory of Monsters*, pp. 322–33.

23   *Ibid.*, pp. 110, 113, 215.

24   Prunier, *From Genocide to Continental War*, p. 306.

25   Interview with Lacaille.

26   Small Arms Survey, 'Demobilization in the DRC'; Sean McFate, 'The Link Between DDR and SSR in Conflict-Affected Countries', United States Institute for Peace, Special Report 238, May 2010, p. 9.

27   Interviews with Lacaille and Tillon; Vincenza Scherrer, 'The Democratic Republic of the Congo', in *Disarmament, Demobilization and Reintegration and Security Sector Reform: Insights from UN Experience in Afghanistan, Burundi, the Central African Republic and the Democratic Republic of the Congo* (Geneva: DCAF), pp. 152, 161.

28   Council on Foreign Relations, 'The Crisis in Congo', 18 October 2010, http://www.cfr.org/conflict-assessment/crisis-congo/p34848.

29   'What is Aman Leo?', MONUSCO website: http://monusco.unmissions.org/Default.aspx?tabid=10934&language=en-US.

30   Council on Foreign Relations, 'The Crisis in Congo', 18 October 2010, http://www.cfr.org/conflict-assessment/crisis-congo/p34848.

31   UN Resolution 2098: http://www.un.org/en/ga/search/view_doc.asp?symbol=S/RES/2098(2013).

32   'The DRC, Rebel Retreat: Can the Congolese Army Build on a Rare Victory?', *The Economist*, 2 November 2013, p. 55.

33   Stearns, *Dancing in the Glory of Monsters*, p. 323.

34   Thomas Rid, 'Deterrence Beyond the State: The Israeli Experience',

Contemporary Security Policy, vol. 33, no. 1, April 2012, pp. 124–47, p. 136.

35   An early herald of this reorientation: Martin van Creveld, *The Transformation of War* (New York: Simon & Schuster, 1991), pp. 16–18.

36   Joshua L. Gleis and Benedetta Berti, *Hezbollah and Hamas: a Comparative Study* (Baltimore: Johns Hopkins University Press, 2012), pp. 185–6, 192.

37   Daniel Byman, *A High Price: the Triumphs and Failures of Israeli Counterterrorism* (Oxford/New York: Oxford University Press, 2011), pp. 5–6.

38   Rid, 'Deterrence Beyond the State', p. 125.

39   Avraham Shalom interview. Dror Moreh, director, *The Gatekeepers* (Cinephil/Sony Picture Classics, 2012), 19:25 minutes.

40   Yezid Sayigh, 'A Non-State Actor as Coercer and Coerced: The PLO in Lebanon, 1969–1976', in Lawrence Freedman (ed.), *Strategic Coercion: Concepts and Cases* (Oxford: Oxford University Press, 1998), pp. 212–48.

41   Ami Ayalon interview. Dror Moreh, director, *The Gatekeepers*, 45:30 minutes; see also Byman, *A High Price*, p. 85.

42   Yezid Sayigh, 'Palestine's Prospects', *Survival: Global Politics and Strategy*, vol. 42, no. 4, Winter 2000–2001, pp. 5–19, p. 9.

43   Yassin quoted in Zeki Chehab, *Inside Hamas: The Untold Story of the Militant Islamic Movement* (New York: Nation Books, 2007), p. 23.

44   Byman, *A High Price*, pp. 142–62.

45   Alastair Crooke, 'In Search of Respect at the Table: Hamas ceasefires 2001–03', in Robert Ricigliano, *Choosing to Engage: Armed Groups and Peace Processes* (London: Conciliation Resources, Accord Publication, 2005), pp. 76–9.

46   Roland Friedrich and Arnold Luethold (eds), *Entry-points to Palestinian Security Sector Reform* (Geneva: DCAF, 2007).

47   Byman, *A High Price*, p. 190.

48   Gershon Baskin, *The Negotiator: Freeing Gilad Shalit from Hamas* (Milford/London/Jerusalem: 2013); 'Hamas head sent message to Netanyahu asking for restraint', *Times of Israel*, 18 February 2014.

49   Byman, *A High Price*, p. 254.

50   Avraham Shalom interview. Dror Moreh, director, *The Gatekeepers*, 17:40 minutes.

51   Ami Ayalon interview. Dror Moreh, director, *The Gatekeepers*, 71:00 minutes.

52   Maoz, *Defending the Holy Land*, pp. 499–543; Byman, *A High Price*, pp. 346–78; Rid, 'Deterrence Beyond the State', pp. 124–47.

53   Maoz, *Defending the Holy Land*, p. 479.

54   Avi Dichter interview. Dror Moreh, director, *The Gatekeepers*, 89:10 minutes.

CONCLUSION

In all of the cases, governments opened a political track because they could not meet their objectives via the security track alone. The speed and enthusiasm with which they resorted to negotiations varied considerably. The differences derived in part from their relative strength and whether their primary interest was victory or survival.

In Northern Ireland, the UK government used military force to create the conditions in which a political process could take root. Ultimately, it persuaded the IRA that the IRA's objectives could not be secured on the battlefield, thus establishing the vital precondition for a political compromise. Progress was slow and halting, and over time the UK government struggled to calibrate the level of military force applied. The UK approach was concurrent, with political initiatives often complementing a constant military element. However, it is important not to exaggerate the strategic coherence of the UK approach: trial-and-error was readily apparent, and luck played a role too.

The Sri Lankan state's struggle with the Tamil Tigers varied between concurrency and a sequential approach to fighting and negotiating. Ceasefires were part of the narrative of the conflict. At times, Sri Lanka sought to use military force to create the conditions for a negotiated solution – and it came close to achieving this, only to be thwarted by domestic political factors. In the end, the objectives of the principal combatants were not reconciled and the state achieved victory on the battlefield. In this endeavour, negotiations proved cynically useful, buying the military time to prepare and helping the government to temporarily ease the restrictions on its behaviour imposed by the international community.

The case of Colombia highlights the increased complexity when the state actor does not have a monopoly on the use of force and its opponent is not united and has the support of a foreign patron. The actions of paramilitaries and the autonomy of the military for a long time precluded the development of a coherent approach towards the Revolutionary Armed Forces of Colombia (FARC). The watershed, visible in retrospect, was when the Colombia army began to be used in service of a more focused negotiation strategy, after the state's coercive capabilities had been augmented by US assistance. This enabled the Colombian government to pursue a concurrent approach that yielded significant gains, where in the past a sequential approach (ceasefires then fighting) had failed. As with the case of Northern Ireland, it is important not to exaggerate the strategic coherence of the government's approach: even between Uribe and his nominated successor Santos, there were important differences.

Turkey's struggle with the Kurdistan Workers' Party (PKK) likewise underscores the difficulties when the military dominates objective-setting and policymaking. Ozal was the first civilian leader to demonstrate the advantages of a concurrent approach when allied to a more flexible stance with regard to the outcome; in the wake of his death, the window of opportunity for a political solution closed for the best part of a decade. The availability to the PKK of foreign sanctuaries and sympathisers made the Turkish military's task harder, while the nature of the Turkish state cast doubt on whether Ankara and the PKK could find common political ground. At times, Turkish policymakers have married the security and political tracks skilfully; but the hopes that the negotiations that began in 2013 engendered have at the time of writing been largely extinguished.

Russia responded to Chechnya's secessionist challenge with military force in the 1990s, with disastrous results for the republic's population, the Russian public and the Russian state. In 1999 Moscow rejected politics and applied greater force, regaining territory. Yet to secure an outcome that could be presented as a victory, the Russian state applied a selective approach: it embraced and supported Akhmad Kadyrov, while fighting other elements. Ultimately, Moscow placed responsibility for securing Chechnya on its local allies and conferred a large degree of autonomy on the republic. Moscow eventually settled on a selective and concurrent approach that underlined its strategic adaptability and flexibility with regard to outcome – although it could be argued that greater security in Chechnya was purchased at the cost of insecurity in neighbouring territories.

Pakistan adopted a selective approach to the insurgent groups it confronted in the wake of the September 2001 attacks on the US and the subsequent invasion of Afghanistan. Given the fragmented nature of the insurgency and the state's limitations, this was the only viable approach. In this instance, the constraining effect of a foreign ally with incongruent objectives loomed large: the US wrecked agreements that Pakistan concluded with militant groups in 2004. Although Pakistan's approach was step by step, rather than strategic, it was skilful and reasonably successful in its use of negotiating and fighting, as a way of weakening the insurgent challenge and building its own position.

The struggle with the Taliban in Afghanistan underlines the difficulties when a government is internally divided and weak, and therefore beholden to foreign allies with different objectives. The lack of unity on the state side was mirrored on the part of the insurgents, who were factionalised. Foreign sanctuaries for the insurgency and the support of foreign patrons were also complicating factors. There was little strategic coherence to the approach, as exemplified by the disputes between Holbrooke and Petraeus (and Obama and Karzai). Negotiations had only a small role to play in the counter-insurgency campaign, while Karzai used them for his personal political interests. Opportunities to exploit military superiority in search of a political agreement were lost. By the time the US was ready to negotiate in earnest, the Taliban had calculated that victory was within sight.

The post-invasion authorities in Iraq, working in occasionally fractious tandem with their allies, pursued a selective approach to the country's insurgency from the outset. In the face of passive and active external support for the insurgency, this eventually yielded a shaky political solution, with marked improvements in security by 2011. Key to this was a series of accommodations that narrowed the range of challengers to the state, partly through political accommodations. That enabled Maliki and the US to focus on recalcitrant elements. However, the strategic coherence of the approach should not be exaggerated: luck played a role, and the political construct proved not to be durable as Maliki's sectarianism undermined the political balance on which improved security had rested.

In the Democratic Republic of the Congo (DRC), the state that emerged from the April 2002 Sun City Agreement was weak and fragmented, while its opponents were also divided, although some of them enjoyed foreign support. As a result, the government had no choice but to pursue a selective approach, fighting some groups and accommodating others; perhaps unsurprisingly, it scored few successes beyond survival. This only changed in 2013–14, when the UN in effect boosted the state's coercive capacity. Thereafter, the government mixed fighting and negotiating to good effect, again with the assistance of the international community, which pressured Rwanda into a more constructive posture.

Israel, by contrast, had far greater resources at its disposal as it faced the choice of how to shape a response to the Palestinian insurgency. Israel prioritised the military lever in its dealings with the Pakistan Liberation Organization (PLO) for many years, but later practised a selective approach by accommodating Fatah and fighting Hamas – although it agreed short-term truces with the latter group in 2001–03. Israel's military strength arguably undermined its ability to forge a strategic approach, and the structure of Israeli domestic politics was such that the conviction never took firm hold that a lasting peace was possible. Thus, Israel has focused on managing the insurgency rather than resolving it through a political process supported by military action.

Developing an analytical framework

The diverse cases show the utility of using a common framework to analyse these conflicts and the challenge of managing the mix of negotiating and fighting. It begins with a consideration of the nature of the conflict and the interests that are at stake. Is there scope for a mutually acceptable solution? Often at the outset the answer is negative, but over time, as some of the cases demonstrate, it can change.

Then the focus shifts to the primary parties in the conflict. Is the state authority in control of the military and political levers, such that it is in a position to pursue a coherent approach? Some governments do not have full control over the military; others struggle to keep notionally sympathetic paramilitary forces in check. On the other side of the conflict, is there unity among military formations and is there a united political entity that can act as a credible negotiating partner?

The picture is further complicated if external parties are involved. Foreign patrons can enable and/or constrain a government facing an armed group, depending on their own resources and the congruence of approach regarding objectives and methods. The same applies to foreign patrons of the non-state armed group. Neighbouring states can also be a passive factor, through the provision of sanctuaries in the form of poorly governed territory.

Once the parties to the conflict and their interests are established, consideration turns to how the state is acting: sequentially (alternating between fighting and negotiating), concurrently (fighting and negotiating at the same time) or selectively (fighting with some insurgents, negotiating with others). As with the other analytical aspects, it is important to track any changes in approach over time.

The cases suggest that it is easiest for a state to reach a final goal in cases where there are just two primary actors. In the case of Northern Ireland, for instance, the UK had control of the military and political tracks, was not greatly troubled by paramilitaries, and faced a predominantly united opponent in IRA–Sinn Féin. The more primary actors are involved, the more difficult it is to achieve a lasting military or political solution because of problems of coordination and management, as well as differences in objectives.

The same applies to the number of secondary actors, albeit with a caveat. As the examples of Afghanistan and Pakistan underline, weak governments often find themselves at cross purposes with allies on which they rely. The same can apply to non-state armed groups with foreign sponsors. From the perspective of articulating clear goals and the effective management of state policy, including the mix of fighting and negotiating, it is better for a state to be unencumbered. The cases of Colombia and the DRC illustrate this, where external assistance was vital to building the state's coercive capacity and thus enabling a more effective concurrent approach. In cases in which the interests of the external party are largely or wholly consistent with those of the government, the difficulties of articulating clear goals and developing a plan of action may be mitigated.

Viewed from this perspective, it is evident that the Northern Ireland case – which is often put forward as a textbook example of solving a protracted internal conflict – is an outlier. It is one of the very few conflicts in the past 40 years where the primary state actor is a G7 state with extensive resources, in full control of the military and political tracks. There was little complicating external involvement in the conflict. The issue at dispute was, ultimately, one that was amenable to a political solution. And in IRA–Sinn Féin, the UK faced a cohesive opponent that was eventually prepared to accept a political compromise.

The case of Colombia, which at the time of writing is negotiating a comprehensive peace deal with FARC, is more representative of the challenges facing a government that tries to end an insurgency through a mix of fighting and negotiating. For many years Colombia struggled to marry the political and military tracks, and in particular to control the military and paramilitaries. The stakes of the conflict were enormous (80,000 dead versus fewer than 4,000 in Northern Ireland). Bogotá relied on a foreign patron as it sought to build its coercive capacity, and it faced not one insurgency but three or more. Its principal opponent, FARC, enjoyed sanctuaries in Ecuador and on occasion the support of the Venezuelan and Ecuadorean governments.

Many states can draw encouragement from the example of Colombia, because from a difficult starting point it is within sight of meeting its ultimate objective. However, not every government can realistically aspire to ending an insurgency through some combination of fighting and negotiating. In the case of Pakistan and the DRC, the primary government objective is survival, with the hope that eventually a series of accommodations and an increase in state capacity will make a more ambitious objective feasible. Israel presents a different type of conflict: one where, in the domestic political realm, it is easier to contain the security threat than to press for a political settlement that might tackle the root cause.

With regard to approach, the cases suggest that a concurrent approach is more likely to yield results than a sequential one. Selectivity is often a choice forced upon relatively weak governments and is less useful for the achievement of final goals, because it involves dealing with the challenge in a piece-meal fashion. However, it has to be acknowledged that interim goals are often the best that can be achieved and that it can take decades to progress beyond them.

No exit

Many states oscillate between security and political approaches, with no end in sight. Wars in Turkey, Colombia and Afghanistan have at times exemplified this sort of strategic drift. A degree of containment is achieved with security measures, but victory or a political settlement remain elusive. The inability to achieve victory on the battlefield is often what impels a state to open a political track in the first place. Negotiations have their own challenges.

Peace processes and political processes are not identical. Politics may well carry on without accommodating armed groups. Some states simply never countenance negotiations, and may never be forced to, if they can partially contain and live with the threat. And some armed groups are especially hard to talk to. Not every violent movement undergoes a political metamorphosis akin to Sinn Féin, or indeed to Nelson Mandela, whose 1960s involvement in 'Spear of the Nation', the armed wing of the African National Congress (ANC), saw him jailed for 27 years by South Africa's apartheid regime. The notion of negotiating with ISIS seems fanciful.

Including armed groups in political processes can be painstaking work. Firstly, there has to be an identifiable leadership to talk to. Next, preparatory, preferably secret, communications are required to establish basic terms of discussion. 'Backchannels can be useful to feel out positions on both sides but they are not usually strong enough to take the full weight of a negotiation', observes Powell.[1] As the leaked 2010 Oslo recording of Turkey's PKK talks showed, it is hard to secretly build a foundation for a formal peace process.

Doing so requires tempering moral opprobrium. Talks may ultimately have to acknowledge that the roots, if not the methods, of an armed group's struggle have some justification. This is hard to accept when blood has been spilled. Then there are legal barriers to overcome that may have been put in place to sanction and ostracise the group. These can range from bans in domestic law, to US and EU designations as 'terrorist organisations', and UN proscription of individuals linked to terror. Broaching dialogue with armed groups, and then sustaining it, requires states to navigate a range of practical, moral, political and legal hurdles.

Even if a negotiation process gets under way it can be tough to secure a deal. This is evident even in 'simple' scenarios with a single armed group and minimal impact from spoilers. In Northern Ireland, progress was touch and go for years. The difficulties multiply in scenarios taking place in fragile regions and featuring many more parties. The difficulties inherent in state–armed group negotiations can increase the temptation – for all sides – to engage only for cosmetic benefits. Showing others that politics is being given a chance can give cover to states that still harbour desires for military progress (as with Sri Lanka). An armed group may negotiate merely to buy time for rebuilding or to continue to benefit from a war economy that it dominates.[2] The Taliban's approach to talks puts the movement in this category.

A 'wait-and-see' approach is common, no parties being willing to stake too much on dialogue, beyond the limited aim of a cessation in hostilities. Many factors have to fall into place for governments and armed groups to see mutual gain in securing a peace settlement. There must be sufficient will on both sides for a peace process to gain momentum. There must be flexibility to step away from maximalist demands. Spoilers on all sides must be restrained and other factions dealt with.

Policy insights

The strategic art of engaging armed groups sits above the separate logics of security measures and political processes. Political tracks, whether they involve bargaining with or bypassing armed groups, mean little if divorced from security tracks. Conversely, concomitant political processes are essential to embed the gains made in countering and containing the violence. In many instances, states fight and negotiate at the same time. The challenge lies in achieving the right mix and adjusting it as necessary over time. The case studies reflect the difficulties of doing this in practice. Security and political tracks progress according to their own timescales and logic, and so can drift apart or then undermine each other. Effective strategy rests on decision-makers not adopting a partisan approach to the tools at their disposal. Each track must be considered in its own right and in the context of the other activities.[3] Indeed, the essence of a strategy exists in the means of its implementation. As Professor Colin Gray notes: 'All strategy has to be done by tactics, and all tactical effort has some strategic effect, but not all such effort reflects, expresses, and enables purposeful strategy.'[4]

Beyond this general point, the case studies underline several useful lessons. Firstly, unity of command is vital. Governments that do not control the military and political levers invariably fail to achieve their objectives. The main problem is control of the military, particularly in weak or transitional states. Yet even in the case of the US in Afghanistan, there was a failure to break down the barriers between soldiers and diplomats who, if not exactly working at cross purposes, were pursuing different plans.

Secondly, patience is vital. The political and military tracks, especially when the former is supported by economic development measures, can take years to deliver the decisive change that creates the possibility for bringing an insurgency to a definitive end. Premature efforts to do so can set back progress, and the groundwork will in many cases take several government or presidential terms before an opportunity emerges.

Thirdly, flexibility and decisiveness is vital too. Governments that regularly reassess the political and military situation, plus their objectives and those of their opponents, are most likely to spot opportunities when they emerge. The passage of time can alter what is acceptable for one or more sides with regard to means and ends. When opportunities emerge, they can only be exploited by decisive leadership. This book recounts several instances of missed opportunities.

Fourthly, reshaping the external environment is often a prerequisite for a government to end an insurgency. One aspect of this concerns changes that strengthen the state or loosen the constraints upon it. The obvious examples are UN support for the government of the DRC and US military aid to Colombia, both of which increased the state's military capacity; and the steps taken by the government of Sri Lanka to restrict the flow of information from the area of its military operations during the decisive offensives, which limited the scope for international pressure to be applied on the Sri Lankan government to exercise restraint.

The other aspect concerns measures to weaken an insurgent group or reduce support for it. For example, Turkey succeeded in reducing the level of foreign support for the PKK and denying it sanctuaries in Syria; the UK government likewise was able to press the US to restrict the flow of funding to Sinn Féin/the IRA from Irish American communities. An active regional policy also enabled Colombia at times to place limits on the assistance that Venezuela in particular afforded FARC.

Fifthly, pushing for a particular solution does not necessarily preclude eventually arriving at a difficult one. It is common sense to conclude that if a military seeks to decapitate the leadership of an insurgency, particularly with the objective of fracturing it, then the possibilities for a negotiated solution will diminish or disappear entirely. Yet there is enough evidence in the case studies to suggest that – in the context of struggles that can run for decades – efforts to secure a military victory do not preclude the possibility of a political settlement. Likewise, a concerted push for a political solution does not rule out the possibility of victory eventually being secured on the battlefield, as the Sri Lankan example underlines.

It follows, therefore, that a theory of victory will be contingent on what is feasible to achieve and on the unsatisfying and partial progress often made when facing armed groups. Muddling through may be the only option for a government fixated simply on survival. Even governments in stronger positions may well end up managing rather than resolving matters. While a definitive end may eventually come, armed-group confrontations can risk being generational undertakings. As one phase of violence ends it may contain the seeds of future dissatisfaction and resurgent war. Successive generations of policymakers will almost certainly inherit the bad legacies of the policies of those that preceded them.

Consequently, the journey may well prove to be more important than the destination in these encounters. As Professor Lawrence Freedman explains, it can be misleading to conceive of strategy as moving towards an end point; strategy is more usefully thought of as finding a pragmatic way of moving from one step to the next, with each step presenting another set of problems, and another set of decisions to make.[5] This being so, the inadvertent consequences of today's actions must be factored into tomorrow's conditions.

If this sounds overly pessimistic, it need not preclude thinking about what progress actually looks like. Strategic progress in wars with armed groups is best thought of as influencing the overall trajectory of the situation. The immediate aim in most of these confrontations is, in the first instance, to reduce the scale and frequency of armed-group violence. Even if the ultimate aim then differs, states are, in general, seeking to exert control over the situation. If the levels of insecurity remain low, this becomes easier to do.

There are as many theories of victory as there are wars with armed groups. There is no 'magic formula' for getting the policy mix 'right'. Each state will engage armed groups in ways that accord with its unique goals, values, capabilities and partnerships, and based on whether the encounter is unfolding at home or abroad. In all cases, strategies can stand and fall on an aptitude and ability to employ the separate streams of engagement in a mutually supportive manner. In this regard at least, one can discern the relevance of the lessons from one scenario to another, in order to shed light on the strategic art of confronting armed groups.

Notes

1   Jonathan Powell, *Great Hatred, Little Room*: *Making Peace in Northern Ireland* (London: Bodley Head, 2009), p. 242.

2   Anthony Vinci, *Armed Groups and the Balance of Power: The International Relations of Terrorists, Warlords and Insurgents* (London/New York: Routledge, 2008).

3   Lawrence Freedman, *Strategy: A History* (New York: Oxford University Press, 2013), pp. 242–5.

4   Colin S. Gray, 'Strategy: Some Notes for a User's Guide', *Infinity Journal*, vol. 2, no. 2, March 2012.

5   Freedman, *Strategy: A History*, pp. 541, 611.

INDEX